FAMILY
Seasons

Other Books by Claudio and Pamela Consuegra

Family Faith

Help! I'm a Parent

Making Jesus My Best Friend:
Baptismal Preparation for Younger Children

FAMILY Seasons

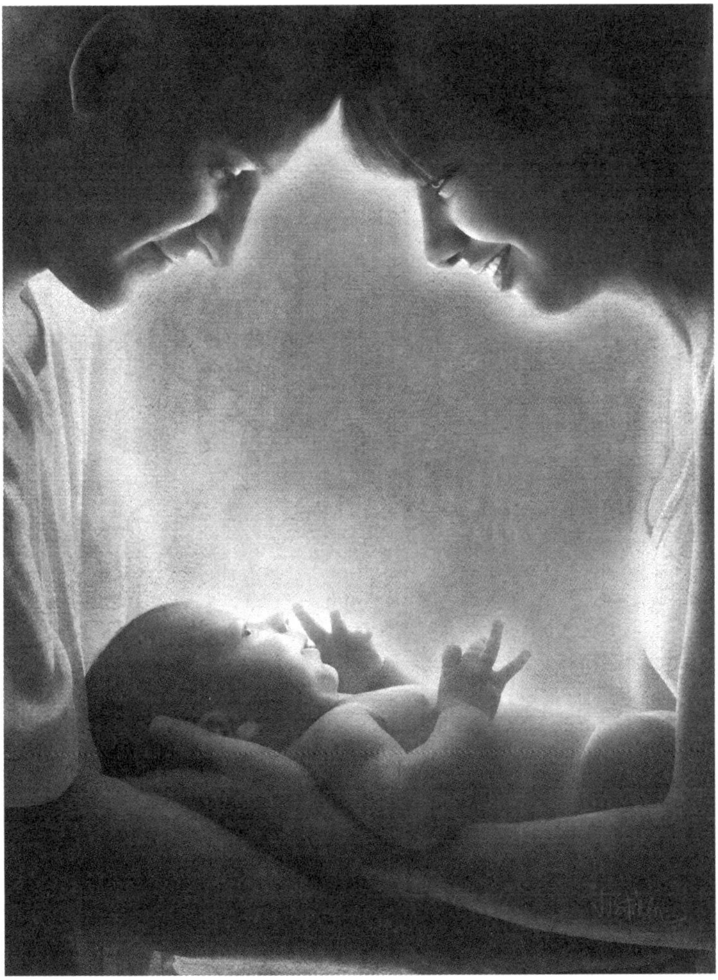

CLAUDIO AND PAMELA CONSUEGRA

Publishing Association
Nampa, Idaho | www.pacificpress.com

Cover design and resources from Lars Justinen

Copyright © 2018 by Pacific Press® Publishing Association
Printed in the United States of America
All rights reserved

The authors assume full responsibility for the accuracy of all facts and quotations as cited in this book.

Unless otherwise noted, all Scripture quotations are from the New King James Version®. Copyright © 1982 by Thomas Nelson. Used by permission. All rights reserved.
Scripture quotations marked ASV are from the American Standard Version of the Bible.
Scripture quotations marked CEV are from the Contemporary English Version®. Copyright © 1995 American Bible Society. All rights reserved.
Scripture quotations marked ESV are from The Holy Bible, English Standard Version® (ESV®), copyright © 2001 by Crossway, a publishing ministry of Good News Publishers. Used by permission. All rights reserved.
Scripture quotations marked GNT are from the Good News Translation® (Today's English Version, Second Edition). Copyright © 1992 American Bible Society. All rights reserved.
Scripture quotations marked KJV are from the King James Version of the Bible.
Scripture taken from *The Message*. Copyright © 1993, 1994, 1995, 1996, 2000, 2001, 2002. Used by permission of NavPress Publishing Group.
Scripture quotations marked NASB are from the NEW AMERICAN STANDARD BIBLE®, copyright © 1960, 1962, 1963, 1968, 1971, 1972, 1973, 1975, 1977, 1995 by the Lockman Foundation. Used by permission. www.lockman.org
Scripture quotations marked NIV are from THE HOLY BIBLE, NEW INTERNATIONAL VERSION®. Copyright © 1973, 1978, 1984, 2011 by Biblica, Inc.® Used by permission. All rights reserved worldwide.
Scripture quotations marked RSV are from the Revised Standard Version of the Bible, copyright © 1946, 1952, 1971 by the Division of Christian Education of the National Council of the Churches of Christ in the United States of America. Used by permission. All rights reserved.

Additional copies of this book are available for purchase by calling toll-free 1-800-765-6955 or by visiting http://www.adventistbookcenter.com.

Library of Congress Cataloging-in-Publication Data
Names: Consuegra, Claudio, author. | Consuegra, Pamela, author.
Title: Family seasons / Claudio and Pamela Consuegra.
Description: Nampa, Idaho : Pacific Press Publishing Association, [2018]
Identifiers: LCCN 2018027444| ISBN 9780816364305 | ISBN 9780816364312 (ebook)
Subjects: LCSH: Families—Religious aspects—Christianity.
Classification: LCC BV4526.3 .C658 2018 | DDC 249—dc23 LC record available at https://lccn.loc.gov/2018027444

October 2018

Table of Contents

Introduction		7
Chapter 1	The Seasons of Life	11
Chapter 2	Seasons to Choose	19
Chapter 3	Seasons of Change	29
Chapter 4	Seasons of Being Alone	37
Chapter 5	Seasons of Wisdom	45
Chapter 6	Seasons of Marriage	55
Chapter 7	Seasons of Unity	65
Chapter 8	Seasons of Parenting	75
Chapter 9	Seasons of Loss	85
Chapter 10	Seasons of Conflict	93
Chapter 11	Seasons of Faith	101
Chapter 12	Seasons of Witnessing	111
Chapter 13	The Final Season	119
Epilogue	Eternity With Jesus	127

Introduction

Even though we are accustomed to special effects in television and movies, it is difficult to imagine what Creation week must have been like. Hollywood can hardly reproduce the wonder of God speaking the world into existence. From total darkness and chaos to the beauty of pure air, crystal-clear waters, and perfect harmony between God's creatures—it must have been spectacular. The six most significant days in Earth's history were crowned with the creation of Adam and Eve, the first human family. God proudly surveyed His handiwork and declared it very good, "so the evening and the morning were the sixth day" (Genesis 1:31).

The capstone He placed on His signature work was the first seventh-day Sabbath. "The great Jehovah, when He had laid the foundations of the earth, when He had dressed the whole world in its garb of beauty, and created all the wonders of the land and the sea, instituted the Sabbath day and made it holy."[1]

Everything and everyone were perfect. If sin had not entered the world, Adam and Eve would have lived forever and would still revel in countless generations and unnumbered descendants, all happy and healthy, enjoying God's creation and never becoming sick or dying.

Unfortunately, the story becomes somber when sin enters the

world. The picture of perfection devolves into high drama and nightmare scenes. Adam and Eve personally witness the decay and death brought on by their sad decision to disobey God. Today's familiar images, which we view as normal, brought heart-wrenching pain to Adam and Eve. "As they witnessed in drooping flower and falling leaf the first signs of decay, Adam and his companion mourned more deeply than men now mourn over their dead. The death of the frail, delicate flowers was indeed a cause of sorrow; but when the goodly trees cast off their leaves, the scene brought vividly to mind the stern fact that death is the portion of every living thing."[2] What should have been an endless cycle of joy became an unending cycle of pain and suffering. Sickness, decay, and death were bequeathed to every human being.

Though a great deal changed after the entrance of sin, what did not change were the sunrise and the sunset. On the fourth day of Creation, God said, " 'Let there be lights in the firmament of the heavens to divide the day from the night; and let them be for signs and seasons, and for days and years; and let them be for lights in the firmament of the heavens to give light on the earth'; and it was so" (verses 14, 15). These celestial markers have marked the days and years for millennia. Farmers plant and reap, people work and rest, all in rhythm with the natural pattern set by these lights—the sun and the moon. Those on the temperate ends of the Northern and Southern Hemispheres experience dramatic changes in temperature when their part of the world moves from the cold of winter to the heat of summer. In more tropical areas, the seasons are marked by the abundance or lack of rain. Lyricist Sheldon Harnick penned this cyclical, seasonal movement:

> Sunrise, sunset, sunrise, sunset
> Swiftly fly the years
> One season following another . . .[3]

We are familiar with the seasons of nature, so it is not

Introduction

surprising that we would notice patterns in our personal lives. In the pages that follow, we will explore the family, its seasons, and how sin derailed God's plan for His creation. Finally, we will review what He has in mind for us until He makes all things good again.

---

1. Ellen G. White, *Christ Triumphant* (Hagerstown, MD: Review and Herald®, 1999), 355.

2. Ellen G. White, *Patriarchs and Prophets* (Mountain View, CA: Pacific Press®, 1958), 62.

3. Sheldon Harnick and Jerry Bock, "Sunrise, Sunset," in *Fiddler on the Roof*, written by Joseph Stein, 1964, https://genius.com/Jerry-bock-sunrise-sunset-lyrics.

CHAPTER 1

The Seasons of Life

As Solomon contemplated life, he penned his profound conclusions in the book of Ecclesiastes. Perhaps knowing that his reign and his life would end one day, he left words of wisdom as a legacy to his children. Since all Scripture is inspired by God and written for our guidance, his wise thoughts are for us as well (see 2 Timothy 3:16; Romans 15:4). Among other important insights, he conveys the perils of pleasure (Ecclesiastes 2), the value of wisdom (Ecclesiastes 7, 9), and most important, the need for a balanced life (Ecclesiastes 7). What ultimately matters, however, is remembering God and obeying His commandments (Ecclesiastes 11, 12).

It is in Ecclesiastes 3 that we find the well-known and oft-quoted words, "There is a time for everything, and a season for every activity under the heavens" (verse 1, NIV). Our lives are not mere coincidence. Events are not happenstance. There is, he writes, an appointed time for everything in life. Some of the seasons come naturally; others arrive unexpectedly. Some changes are gradual, while others are abrupt.

In all of this, there are two promises that must be remembered. First, the seasons are sure. After the floodwaters receded, God promised Noah that

> "While the earth remains,
> Seedtime and harvest,
> Cold and heat,
> Winter and summer,
> And day and night
> Shall not cease" (Genesis 8:22).

Second, and most important, in all the seasons of life, God is by your side. He will never leave you nor forsake you (see Genesis 28:15; Deuteronomy 31:6, 8; Joshua 1:5; Matthew 28:20; Hebrews 13:5). So take heart, no matter the season of your journey, for God is with you.

The seasons begin

From a world of chaos and darkness, God created the earth as a home for humans, animals, and plants. "For He spoke, and it was done; He commanded, and it stood fast" (Psalm 33:9). During the first three days of Creation, God spoke and things happened. There was light, night, and day (Genesis 1:3–5). The atmosphere, vital for the existence of life, enveloped the earth (verses 6, 7). Dry land emerged from the midst of oceans, and the dry land sprouted trees, plants, and grass (verses 9–12).

During the next three days, God made luminaries in the sky (verses 14–19), water creatures and birds (verses 20–22), and land animals of all types, shapes, and sizes (verses 24, 25). On the sixth day, He formed humans after His own image (verses 26–28). Though He could have ordered everything to appear at once, He took His time to create life on Earth, eventually shaping Adam and Eve with His own hands.

As we rush through the Creation account, it is easy to miss some interesting facts. On the first day, God spoke light into existence, but it was not until the fourth day that lights in the firmament were made. This seems strange, but it makes sense to begin creation with light because there could be no life without it. On a deeper level, the physical separation of light from darkness is highly symbolic of the spiritual reality that light and darkness cannot coexist. "I [Jesus] have come as a light into the world, that whoever believes in Me should not abide in darkness" (John 12:46). "God is light and in Him is no darkness at all" (1 John 1:5). God's presence, from the first day of Creation, brought light and life into this world of darkness.

The lights He created on the fourth day, while providing energy and illumination, were also designed to serve a special purpose: "to divide the day from the night; . . . for signs and seasons, and for days and years" (Genesis 1:14). Of course, this perfect world did not know seasons as we know them today. For example, there was no rainy season, since "a mist went up from the earth and watered the whole face of the ground" (Genesis 2:6). Furthermore, the sun, moon, and stars were established as heavenly timepieces to mark the week—from Sabbath to Sabbath—as well as the months and the years. On their journey through space, they would function as gigantic, predictable celestial clocks. Science has confirmed that these heavenly bodies not only mark days, months, and years, they also exert a tremendous influence on the tides, atmosphere, and seasons. Their impact is felt even on human, animal, and vegetable life. God made them for us and for our benefit.

Predictable seasons

Ben Franklin famously quipped, "Nothing can be said to be certain, except death and taxes." Taxes provide income for governments to fund operations and are subject to the whims of lawmakers. Death, on the other hand, comes to all humanity (Ezekiel 18:4; Romans 6:23).

Even Jesus was confronted with the reality of death and taxes. When the disciples asked if they should pay taxes to Caesar, He responded, "Give to Caesar [the government] what belongs to Caesar [taxes], and give to God what belongs to God [our lives]" (Matthew 22:21, NLT). When death stood in His way, He defeated it by raising the son of the widow of Nain (Luke

7:11–17), Jairus's daughter (Mark 5:21–43), and Lazarus (John 11). In the end, He once and for all defeated death by coming back from the dead Himself.

While most matters in life cannot be controlled, the choice to avoid eternal death and accept God's gift of eternal life is yours to make. Jesus made it clear that there is more to life than waiting for death. He told His disciples, "I have come that they may have life, and that they may have it more abundantly" (John 10:10). He also told Martha, Lazarus's sister, "I am the resurrection and the life. He who believes in Me, though he may die, he shall live. And whoever lives and believes in Me shall never die. Do you believe this?" (John 11:25, 26) It is an unsettling thought, but all humanity is moving toward the grave. Without the hope of eternal life, that predictable march can be hopeless and discouraging; but with it, this life is just another step toward eternity.

When the unexpected happens

More than any other biblical figure, Job is known for the difficult and painful trials he endured. We marvel at his faith and patience in the face of tragedy, wondering how we would respond to similar losses. We relate to Job's pain because it reminds us so much of our own. We follow his journey from familial joy to the pit of despair because we have traversed the same dark valley of the shadow of death. When he is finally vindicated by God, we revel in the triumph of justice and fairness, longing for the day when our own injustices will be overturned.

But not all unexpected changes are negative. Scripture records the stories of unanticipated changes that placed individuals in positions of honor and influence. Joseph, after years as a slave and a stint in prison, was promoted by Pharaoh to be his second-in-command (Genesis 41:39–42). Moses, the adopted son of Pharaoh's daughter, had to flee for his life but later emerged as a leader of God's people (Exodus 2, 3). Daniel, the Hebrew worthy, was promoted by Darius the Mede and Cyrus the Persian to top positions in their governments (Daniel 6:28).

The Seasons of Life

Esther, the adopted daughter of her Jewish cousin, became a queen and wife of King Ahasuerus (Esther 2). Galilean fishermen and tax collectors became disciples of Jesus and pillars of the early Christian church (Matthew 10:1–4; Ephesians 2:20). Saul went from persecutor to persecuted, from leader in the Jewish Sanhedrin to leader in the Christian church, from tentmaker to world missionary (Acts 9, 13–28). These heroes and a host of others were unexpectedly disrupted when God called them. Yet during those unexpected seasons in their lives, they responded to God's call, rose to the challenge, and were used in mighty ways.

Transitions

Seasons change gradually, not suddenly. Cold, barren winter gives way to fresh spring flowers and blooming trees. Tepid spring rains evaporate in summer's heat. Autumn's wind and rain sweep summer away and strip trees bare. Soon a chill in the air drives us to warmer clothes, and winter settles in until spring begins a new cycle of seasons.

Calendars assign specific dates to the beginning and the end of each season but the dates of the equinoxes or the solstices do not instantly change the seasons. The transitions are gradual, almost imperceptible.

People also change, slowly and subtly. Jesus' disciples changed as they spent time with Him. They were simple folk, accustomed to the teachings and traditions of their Jewish faith. The Galilean Rabbi moved them as no one ever had, but they were still human and experienced jealousy and conflict (Matthew 20:20–24; Luke 9:46). They seemed to lack faith, and even abandoned Jesus, denying they knew Him (Mark 9:28, 29; Matthew 26:56, 69–74). At the same time, however, they were growing spiritually, and eventually, people recognized that they were different. Even Peter's speech had changed since meeting the Nazarene. This transformation was noted by the Jewish Sanhedrin: they "perceived that they [Peter and John] were uneducated and untrained men. . . . And they realized that they had been with Jesus" (Acts 4:13).

A popular bumper sticker proclaims that "Christians are not perfect, just forgiven." The apostle Paul recognized this truth and pointed out that in the process of growing in Christ there are many battles to fight, and sometimes we lose them. Of his own struggle, he wrote, "For what I am doing, I do not understand. For what I will to do, that I do not practice; but what I hate, that I do" (Romans 7:15). But at the end of his journey, he could also write, "I have fought the good fight, I have finished the race, I have kept the faith" (2 Timothy 4:7). This is what growth in Christ does for us.

Daily we are changed, and even if the transitions are not apparent to us, they are often noticed by others. "The more we contemplate the character of Christ, and the more we experience of His saving power, the more keenly shall we realize our own weakness and imperfection, and the more earnestly shall we look to Him as our strength and our Redeemer."[1]

Interactions

Tropical climates close to the Earth's equator bring more warmer weather than the chill of the North and South Poles. Moving away from the equator, toward the far reaches of the Northern and Southern Hemispheres, the four seasons become more distinct. Each time of year brings its own beauty. The bright colors of autumn contrast with winter's white snow, and spring outdoes them all with its explosion of life. Summer invites people to be outdoors, go for a swim, or simply enjoy the sunshine.

Those living in tropical climates do not worry about slick winter roads or the autumn chill. All year long, they enjoy warmth and sunshine. But even in the tropics, countries with tall mountains can have vastly different climates as one moves from sea level to higher altitudes. Perhaps the writer of Ecclesiastes recognized these differences and drew on the image of seasons to remind us that we should appreciate our differences. Nothing is

The Seasons of Life

gained by comparing ourselves with one another, and the Bible goes out of its way to showcase diverse and unique relationships that helped people negotiate the seasons of life.

Developing relationships is precisely why God created Adam. He said, "It is not good that man should be alone" (Genesis 2:18). After bringing Adam to life, He created an equal partner, Eve, to be his companion. Today each person, whether married or not, needs the encouragement of those around them. The church family in particular plays an important role in the lives of those who are not married, surrounding them with the love and support they need.

Ellen White paints a simple picture of what happens in the family and in the church:

> Picture a large circle, from the edge of which are many lines all running to the center. The nearer these lines approach the center, the nearer they are to one another.
>
> Thus it is in the Christian life. The closer we come to Christ, the nearer we shall be to one another. God is glorified as His people unite in harmonious action.[2]

We need each other in the journey through life. Transitions are inevitable and are often painful, but traveling together makes it easier. Solomon explained,

> Two are better than one,
> Because they have a good reward for their labor.
> For if they fall, one will lift up his companion.
> But woe to him who is alone when he falls,
> For he has no one to help him up.
> Again, if two lie down together, they will keep warm;
> But how can one be warm alone?
> Though one may be overpowered by another, two can withstand him.
> And a threefold cord is not quickly broken (Ecclesiastes 4:9–12).

Family Seasons

The folk singer Harry Chapin wrote about the seasons of life and declared, "All my life's a circle . . ."[3] The Bible, however, goes beyond Chapin's circle of repetition. It describes life as more than a replaying of experiences without end, purpose, and meaning. Each day is a new opportunity to observe God's leading in the journey to heaven and eternity with Him. Through the years, He is moving you forward, always anticipating the next season of life.

For further consideration

1. In what season of life do you find yourself? How satisfied are you in that season? If you are happy, how can you take advantage of this season to help others who may be going through a more difficult time? If you are not happy, what steps can you take to transition to a happier season?

2. How do you prepare for the expected? The unexpected?

3. Read Ecclesiastes 3:1 again. How does the idea of a season for everything shape your perspective on possessions? Make a list of the ten most important things, responsibilities, and people in your life. Prioritize them from the most important to the least important. Are you living according to your priority list? Consult these texts as you make your list: Psalm 37:3; Proverbs 3:27; Luke 6:27, 33; 10:27; 12:34.

---

1. Ellen G. White, *Our Father Cares* (Hagerstown, MD: Review and Herald®, 1991), 291.

2. Ellen G. White, *The Adventist Home* (Washington, DC: Review and Herald®, 1952), 179.

3. Harry Chapin, "Circle," track 2 on *Sniper and Other Love Songs*, Elektra, 1972, https://www.azlyrics.com/lyrics/harrychapin/circle361389.html.

CHAPTER 2

Seasons to Choose

The book of Joshua recounts Israel's miraculous crossing of the Jordan River (Joshua 3, 4), the fall of Jericho (Joshua 6), and the defeat of Ai (Joshua 7, 8). The next fifteen chapters chronicle the Israelites' phenomenal victories and the division of the land into the nine and a half tribes west of the Jordan. In Joshua 23, God "had given rest to Israel," and Joshua was "old, advanced in age" and nearing the end of his leadership career (verse 1). Knowing death was imminent, he called for a meeting of the people to remind them that it was God who "fought for them" (verse 3).

The challenge, as Joshua saw it, was the considerable land and nations that had yet to be conquered. He was unconcerned with God's willingness to lead the conquest but was worried about the Israelites comingling with the people of the land, adopting the worship of their gods, and forgetting the God who had led them to the Promised Land. It is in this context that he takes a strong stand for himself and his family, expressed in some of the most memorable verses of Scripture: "But if you refuse to serve the Lord, then choose today whom you will serve. Would you prefer the gods your ancestors served beyond the Euphrates? Or will it be the gods of the Amorites in whose land you now live? But as for me and my family, we will serve the Lord" (Joshua 24:15, NLT).

Family Seasons

Life is full of choices. Some are simple and routine, while others are life changing. Certain choices not only affect us but carry lasting consequences for other people in our lives. It is encouraging to know that even during these seasons of choice, God remains by our side and tells us, "Be very courageous" (Joshua 23:6).

Free will, free choices

The faith we live by is a personal, individual choice. People may choose to worship many different gods—Vishnu, Mithra, Zeus, power, sex, or money. The Hebrews chose to worship God, or rather, they were chosen by God. While God chose the Hebrews to be His people, they, too, had a choice. After forty years of desert wandering, they stood on the borders of the Promised Land, and Moses reminded them of the many times God had shown them favor. A large multitude, estimated at more than two million men, women, children, and foreigners, never went hungry or thirsty. "Your clothes have not worn out on you, and your sandals have not worn out on your feet" (Deuteronomy 29:5). Moses' final word to them was a call to choose life: "I call heaven and earth as witnesses today against you, that I have set before you life and death, blessing and cursing; therefore choose life, that both you and your descendants may live" (Deuteronomy 30:19).

Even though chosen by God, the choice to serve Him was an individual act. Today some choose not to accept God, much like the rich young ruler who felt the price to follow Jesus was too high (Matthew 19:16–22). Others make a positive choice; sometimes at great cost to themselves. Daniel stood alone and prayed as he always did, ending up in the den of lions (Daniel 6). Matthew left the tax collector's table and a lucrative business to follow Jesus (Matthew 9:9). The woman at Jacob's well told others about Jesus, despite her reputation (John 4).

Following Jesus has not always been an easy decision. Nicodemus, a Jewish leader, had to seek Jesus at night in secret (John 3:1–21). He eventually showed his love for Jesus by trying to protect Him from the other Jewish leaders and by providing myrrh and aloes to anoint His dead body (John 7:50, 51; 19:39). Saul, the persecutor who stood by as Stephen was stoned to death, was later persecuted for being a follower of Jesus (Acts 7:57–8:1; 2 Corinthians 11:24–31).

Making the right choices

Soon after Adam and Eve were created, they were confronted with a momentous choice: remain obedient to God or disobey Him by eating the fruit of the tree of the knowledge of good and evil (Genesis 3). Sadly, they listened to the serpent, ate the forbidden fruit, and suffered the consequences of sin and death (Romans 5:12–21). Our first parents' mistaken choice brought woe and misery, but God did not rescind their free will. On the contrary, He preserved their freedom to make personal choices, which is a privilege we enjoy to this day.

No wonder Ellen White reminds us, "Your entire future will be influenced for good or for evil by the path you now choose."[1] Remembering that God chose us is a powerful incentive to pick the right path. Because of His love, how can we live for ourselves, pursuing our own happiness and success, with no regard for Him or others?

Often, our challenge is not a misunderstanding of God's will or ignorance of His Word; the difficulty lies in not liking what He wants for us—as if we think God is unhappy unless we are miserable. And yet nothing is further from the truth. "For I know the thoughts that I think toward you, says the LORD, thoughts of peace and not of evil, to give you a future and a hope" (Jeremiah 29:11). This is the reason Jesus invites us to join Him: "Come to Me, all you who labor and are heavy laden, and I will give you rest" (Matthew 11:28). He wants the best for His children and is pleased when they bring their needs to Him (Luke 11:9–13).

Choosing friends

Of all the choices we make, few have a more lasting impact than our choice of friends. Ellen White explains, "Everyone will find companions or make them. And just in proportion to the strength of the friendship will be the amount of influence which friends will exert over one another for good or for evil. All will have associates and will influence and be influenced in their turn."[2]

Samson is a notable biblical example of poor judgment in choosing friends. His relationship with Delilah ended up costing him his eyesight, his freedom, and ultimately his life (Judges 16). He would have been much better off had he accepted the truth that "evil company corrupts good habits" (1 Corinthians 15:33).

From a positive perspective, friendships can be an incredible blessing. An extraordinary example of such friendship comes from the ancient city of Syracuse and the lives of two young men named Damon and Pythias:

> They were very good friends, and loved each other so dearly that they were hardly ever seen apart.
>
> Now, it happened that Pythias in some way roused the anger of the tyrant [Dionysius I], who put him in prison, and condemned him to die in a few days. When Damon heard of it, he . . . vainly tried to obtain his friend's pardon and release.
>
> The mother of Pythias was very old, and lived far away from Syracuse with her daughter. When the young man heard that he was to die, he was tormented by the thought of leaving the women alone. In an interview with his friend Damon, Pythias regretfully said that he would die easier had he only been able to bid his mother good-by and find a protector for his sister.
>
> Damon . . . went into the presence of the tyrant, and proposed to take the place of Pythias in prison, and even on the cross, if need be, provided the latter were allowed to visit his relatives once more.
>
> Dionysius had heard of the young men's touching friendship, and hated them both . . . ; yet he allowed

them to change places, warning them both, however, that if Pythias were not back in time, Damon would have to die in his stead.

At first Pythias refused to allow his friend to take his place in prison, but finally he consented, promising to be back in a few days to release him. So Pythias hastened home, found a husband for his sister, and saw her safely married. Then, after providing for his mother and bidding her farewell, he set out to return to Syracuse. . . .

[Through a series of adverse circumstances—raging waters and marauding thieves—Pythias was delayed and did not return at the appointed time.]

Dionysius, in the mean while, had been amusing himself by taunting Damon, constantly telling him that he was a fool to have risked his life for a friend, however dear. To anger him, he also insisted that Pythias was only too glad to escape death, and would be very careful not to return in time.

Damon, who knew the goodness and affection of his friend, . . . repeated again and again that he knew Pythias would never break his word, but would be back in time, unless hindered in some unforeseen way.

The last hour came. The guards led Damon to the place of crucifixion, where he again asserted his faith in his friend, adding, however, that he sincerely hoped Pythias would come too late, so that he might die in his stead.

Just as the guards were about to nail Damon to the cross, Pythias dashed up, pale, bloodstained, and disheveled, and flung his arms around his friend's neck with a sob of relief. For the first time Damon now turned pale, and began to shed tears of bitter regret.

In a few hurried, panting words, Pythias explained the cause of his delay, and, loosing his friend's bonds with his own hands, bade the guards bind him instead.

Dionysius, who had come to see the execution, was so

touched by this true friendship, that for once he forgot his cruelty, and let both young men go free, saying that he would not have believed such devotion possible had he not seen it with his own eyes.³

The Scriptures capture this deep friendship when Solomon writes that "there is a friend who sticks closer than a brother" (Proverbs 18:24). Centuries later, Jesus described the same type of friendship when He said, "This is My commandment, that you love one another as I have loved you. Greater love has no one than this, than to lay down one's life for his friends. You are My friends if you do whatever I command you. No longer do I call you servants, for a servant does not know what his master is doing; but I have called you friends" (John 15:12–15). What a Friend we have in Jesus!

Choosing a life partner

The freedom to choose friends, the freedom to choose life, and the freedom to choose God have always been fundamental to the kingdom of heaven. In His divine wisdom, God gave Adam a life partner who would be a "helper comparable to him" (Genesis 2:20). His joy when he first saw Eve caused him to burst into the first poem ever expressed by a human being:

> "Here is someone like me!
> She is part of my body,
>   my own flesh and bones.
> She came from me, a man.
>   So I will name her Woman!" (Genesis 2:23, CEV).

In creating Adam first, God wanted him to experience the need for human companionship; someone to talk to and to listen to. God said, "It is not good that man should be alone" (verse 18); so God created Eve and gave Adam the best gift ever—his own wife!

Seasons to Choose

In biblical times, and in some cultures today, parents play an important role in the choice of a partner for their child. For example, Abraham sent his servant to find a wife for his son Isaac (Genesis 24). A generation later Isaac and his wife, Rebekah, sent Jacob to find a wife from Rebekah's kin, far away from the women of the region (Genesis 27:46–28:2).

Fortunately, God has left us divine guidance in this area of life. In His Word, He provides the proper steps for choosing a spouse:

1. Understand what makes a good partner (Psalm 37:27; 1 Corinthians 15:33; James 1:23–25).
2. It is best to focus on being a good person rather than being preoccupied with finding the right person to marry. Practice kindness and treating others with respect (Matthew 7:12).
3. Wait until the appropriate time to get married (1 Corinthians 7:36).
4. Marry someone with whom you can share a life of faith and ministry (2 Corinthians 6:14).

Choosing a purpose in life

Like marriage, all choices in life must be based on the fact that God first chose you. He chose Israel, not because they were the largest but because they were the smallest. He simply chose them because He loved them (see Deuteronomy 7:7, 8). Jesus also told His disciples, "I chose you" (John 15:16). Let that thought sink in for a minute—God chose you because He loves you.

When God chose Israel to be His people, He planned to reach all humankind through them. When they failed to fulfill their mission to carry God's love to other peoples, the Christian church was commissioned to preach the gospel "in all the world as a witness to all the nations" (Matthew 24:14). That is why Jesus "chose you and appointed you that you should go and bear fruit, and that your fruit should remain" (John 15:16). At some point in one's experience, the season of choosing a life purpose arrives.

In God's plan, not everyone can be a prophet, a pastor, a teacher, or an evangelist but all are called to ministry. From Creation, God planned for work to be part of life (Genesis 2:15). Later the apostle Paul writes to the Ephesians, "Let him who stole steal no longer, but rather let him labor, working with his hands what is good, that he may have something to give him who has need" (Ephesians 4:28).

Work, according to Paul, should do more than meet our own needs; it should help those in need. No matter what we do for a living, those in need should receive some benefit (Exodus 23:10, 11; Deuteronomy 15:7–11). The danger of making work the center of your life is that it does not bring lasting satisfaction. This was Solomon's conclusion when he reviewed his life's work (Ecclesiastes 2:4–11). He searched for meaning in various projects, and even though they brought him gratification, he saw they were meaningless in the end. In choosing a career, it makes sense to learn from the wisest man who ever lived. Work is a blessing if it is God directed. When you live for Him, He equips and blesses you to accomplish His purpose in your life (Exodus 31:2–11).

From the moment you wake up in the morning until you return to bed at the end of the day, life is a series of choices. "Today I have given you the choice between life and death, between blessings and curses. Now I call on heaven and earth to witness the choice you make. Oh, that you would choose life, so that you and your descendants might live!" (Deuteronomy 30:19, NLT). Choose life!

For further consideration

1. What are the five most important choices you have made in your life? Would you say they have all been in agreement with God's plan for you?

2. Would sharing the story of your mistaken choices be helpful to young people?

3. In an increasingly secular society, how can you be a blessing

and witness to others in your work setting? What are some positive and negative approaches in reaching others with the good news from God?

4. If we only have Christian friends, how will others come to know Jesus? How can we be in the world but not of the world? (See Matthew 10:16.)

---

1. Ellen. G. White, *Mind, Character, and Personality* (Nashville, TN: Southern Pub. Assn., 1977), 2:421.

2. Ellen G. White, *The Adventist Home* (Washington, DC: Review and Herald®, 1952), 455.

3. H. A. Guerber, *The Story of the Greeks* (New York: American Book Co., 1896), 204, 205, 207.

CHAPTER 3

Seasons of Change

"The ants are a people not strong, yet they prepare their food in the summer" (Proverbs 30:25). Solomon wisely calls our attention to the tiny ant and its amazing combination of strength, industry, and teamwork. We marvel at its ability to carry bits of leaves that are much bigger and heavier than its own body. During picnics, ants are a nuisance, but they do not mean to be—they are just looking for food. Instinctively, they know that summer will soon be over and they must prepare for winter. Ants toil today because they understand the needs of tomorrow. Through instinct and past experience, they diligently prepare for the future.

In the same way, we are given time to prepare for future events. Marriage, parenting, and our golden years often gather our careful attention. As life grows long, we make plans for the unwelcome specter of death. From beginning to end, we are preparing for life's changes and, most important, preparing for the return of Jesus. Each season of preparation is important; and if done properly, we and our loved ones will be better off. To delay planning or forgo it completely can bring serious consequences.

Like the ant, we are called to work during the spring and summer of life because winter invariably arrives. That winter could be a financial setback, a disaster, a terminal illness, the loss of a job, or a tragic death. It could be the events of the last days, including death threats and persecution. Whatever it may be, now is the season to prepare for it.

Preparing for marriage

For most things in life, success requires preparation. For example, to gain a coveted driver's license, we read a manual, learn from an instructor, practice via driving sessions, and take required tests. For a career or job, we go to school and devote time to learning the necessary skills. For a trip we check schedules, purchase tickets, and pack our suitcases. But dwarfing all these life events and the preparation they require is the matter of marriage. It is among the most important decisions a person will ever make, yet many fail to prepare for the life-changing moment.

Preparation for marriage starts at an early age as one begins to develop an idea of what a future spouse may be like. Some young people fantasize about the spouse's physical attributes—the color of his eyes or her hair or whether the person will be tall or short. Others imagine more lasting features, such as the spouse's personality, commitment to God, or sense of humor. In the process, many develop unrealistic expectations of marriage and the person they will marry one day.

While fantasizing about a future partner, many young people have drifted into the delusion that marriage will be the answer to all their problems. They may not get along with their parents and imagine that marriage will free them of this stress. Too late they find that marriage is not the answer they hoped it would be and are faced with a whole new set of challenges. Others refuse to believe that divorce could ever happen to them, when it can happen to any of us. These misguided expectations often lead people to disappointment and remorse.

Some couples who are deeply in love believe they will never argue. When conflicts emerge, they become disillusioned with their relationship and abandon it. The reality is that all relationships deal with conflict. It is unrealistic to believe that two healthy people with individual goals, dreams, talents, and gifts will not have disagreements. Even couples who have similar personalities, enjoy the same activities, and share similar values have moments of discord. The issue is not whether you will have disagreements but rather the manner in which you will handle those struggles. Dealing appropriately with conflict is crucial for the health of your marriage and your family.

Another unrealistic expectation some people have is in believing that their loved one will change once they are married. This prospect is not the product nor the goal of marriage. Any attempt at coercion is not only a lack of respect for the other person but also an ongoing source of conflict. While marriage does change us, hopefully for the better, we need to ask God to begin the change with us. At the same time, while we may pray that God will affect change in our spouse, we should not take it upon ourselves to be His instrument of that change. Commit your spouse to God, pray for him or her, and allow Him to work in your spouse's heart as He has in yours.

One of the most serious unrealistic expectations for couples is the belief they can work out spiritual differences once they are married. Unfortunately, people rarely change, and spiritual differences can create some of the most difficult and heartbreaking problems a marriage can face. When partners are reared in different faiths, it is not only difficult to worship together, but it is difficult to raise children together. In which faith tradition will the children be trained? For these reasons, God knows that the union of a believer and nonbeliever is difficult and counsels against it in 2 Corinthians 6:14. Matters of faith and other potential areas of conflict should be addressed early in the relationship, before engagement and certainly before the wedding day.

Preparing for parenting
"Children are a heritage from the LORD, the fruit of the womb is a reward" (Psalm 127:3). The birth of a child is cause for

celebration, and when parents are surrounded by their children, their hearts are filled with warmth and love. "Like arrows in the hand of a warrior, so are the children of one's youth. Happy is the man who has his quiver full of them" (Psalm 127:4, 5).

Hannah and Elkanah, Manoah and his wife, Zacharias and Elizabeth, and the virgin Mary were entrusted with special children from God (1 Samuel 1:27; Judges 13:3–7, Luke 1:5, 6, 13–17, 39–45, 46–55, 76–79). Their sons would play important roles in the life of Israel and in the world. These parents did not take their responsibility lightly but instead did everything in their power to be good parents, providing a healthy growth environment for their children.

Those nine months before birth must have been a season of intense prayer; a time to study the Bible prophecies and be reminded of God's loving care; a time to take care of themselves and the health of their unborn child. Of Samson's mother, we're told, "When the Lord would raise up Samson as a deliverer of his people, he enjoined upon the mother correct habits of life before the birth of her child. And the same prohibition was to be imposed, from the first, upon the child; for he was to be consecrated to God as a Nazarite from his birth."[1]

Because a mother carries her baby from conception to birth, it rests on her to take care of herself in order to benefit the child.

> The mother who is a fit teacher for her children must, before their birth, form habits of self-denial and self-control; for she transmits to them her own qualities, her own strong or weak traits of character. The enemy of souls understands this matter much better than do many parents. He will bring temptation upon the mother, knowing that if she does not resist him, he can through her affect her child. The mother's only hope is in God. She may flee to Him for grace and strength. She will not seek help in vain. He will enable her to transmit to her offspring qualities that will help them to gain success in this life and to win eternal life.[2]

Seasons of Change

Preparing for old age

We have often heard the old adage that "time flies." Yesterday we were children, today adults, and tomorrow seniors. We suddenly find ourselves in our golden years. In some countries, government programs and institutions care for the elderly. In other cultures, support for aging parents is left to the children. In most cases, however, people do not want to be a burden to their children and make plans accordingly.

If you are at this stage of life and making these plans, a careful review of the issues below will enable you to better prepare for the last decades of life. Take a moment and reflect on how you can make the future easier and more enjoyable for both you and your family.

- *Finances.* Save for retirement, and plan to have enough money to thrive in old age. Prepare a will or trust, leaving clear directions for the distribution of your assets when you die.
- *Health care.* Have health insurance coverage. Keep your health and life insurance policy information stored in a safe place so that loved ones can find it when needed.
- *End-of-life wishes.* In an emergency, "such as a heart attack, stroke, major injury, or terminal illness," it may be too late to make important decisions about your life. Make sure advance directives are in place: "a durable power of attorney, a living will, and other documents that state your end-of-life wishes." These documents "can save you and your family unneeded stress in a time of crisis."
- *Care for yourself.* The day may come when you nor your loved ones are able to handle your care. Before that time arrives, "make decisions about potential living arrangements, like a nursing home or assisted living facility, hospice care, home health care, and other available care options."
- *Your home.* Will your home be easily accessible if you have

physical limitations in old age? For instance, having stairs to climb may become challenging. From a safety standpoint, it may be wise to think about modifications or remodeling that will maximize mobility. If renovations are not feasible, you may want to move to a home that will be easier to get around.[3]

Preparing for death

If we live long enough, we will suffer through the death of a loved one. King David lost several of his children (2 Samuel 12:15–23; 13:28–30; 18:32, 33); Mary and Martha lost their brother Lazarus (John 11); and Esau and Jacob lost their father (Genesis 35:29). Those who have gone through the experience will say that no pain hurts like the death of a child. Marriages often fail after such an event. Others say that the most traumatic event in life is the death of a spouse. With the loss of child, a couple can turn to each other for strength and comfort; but with the death of a spouse, the remaining partner is left with no consolation.

In the wider circle of life, we may become aware of a friend's impending death or an ailing loved one. If we can learn anything from Job's friends, it is this: they came to see him; they sat with him in silence; and for seven days and seven nights, they "saw that his grief was very great" (Job 2:13). Sometimes just sitting with someone may be the best thing you can do. People going through a terminal illness often have no one to visit with, no one to just be present, and no one to listen. In the last season of life, your presence may be the greatest gift you can give.

Preparing for Christ's return

Nothing in life is as important as preparing for the soon return of Jesus. Christian believers in the church of Thessalonica had many questions about His return, and there was plenty of confusion about the matter. Unlike today, they did not have the New Testament to consult. If they did, they might have read Jesus' promise, "And if I go and prepare a place for you, I will come again and receive you to Myself; that where I am, there you may be also" (John 14:3). Or they would have been assured by Paul that he was "looking for the blessed hope and glorious appearing of our great God and Savior Jesus Christ" (Titus 2:13).

Paul and Jesus often spoke about His return, and Jesus warned us to stay alert and remain faithful (Luke 12:35–48). He also urged us to be watchful and pray always (Matthew 24:42–44; Luke 21:36). Years later, Paul would add that we should be worried for nothing (Philippians 4:5, 6).

These admonitions are reassuring, but they can also be overwhelming. Does anyone have it completely together? Hardly. That is why it is comforting to know that even when we turn our backs on God and choose to live life on our own terms, He does not turn away from us. He has pledged that "if we confess our sins, He is faithful and just to forgive us our sins and to cleanse us from all unrighteousness" (1 John 1:9).

This is why the Bible urges us to "come boldly to the throne of grace, that we may obtain mercy and find grace to help in time of need" (Hebrews 4:16). What a promise! Grace is only a prayer away, and you can be "confident of this very thing, that He who has begun a good work in you will complete it until the day of Jesus Christ" (Philippians 1:6).

For further consideration

1. If you could turn back the clock, what would you do differently before you married? If you are single and believe marriage is in God's plans for you, what can you do to increase the chances of having a lasting relationship with your future spouse?

2. If you have parenting experience, what advice do you have for those who plan to have children?

3. Make a list of encouraging Bible texts you can lean on as you prepare for the second coming of Jesus.

---

1. Ellen G. White, *Christian Temperance and Bible Hygiene* (Battle Creek, MI: Good Health Pub., 1890), 37, 38.

Family Seasons

2. Ellen G. White, *Counsels on Diet and Foods* (Washington, DC: Review and Herald®, 1938), 219.

3. Diana Rodriguez, "Planning for Your Future," Everyday Health, last updated July 8, 2008, https://www.everydayhealth.com/longevity/future-planning.aspx.

CHAPTER 4

Seasons of Being Alone

"Man was not made to dwell in solitude; he was to be a social being."[1] By the sixth day of Creation, God had completed the perfect home for His children. He then formed Adam with His own hands and in His own image (Genesis 1:27). Adam's first task was to name all the animals God had made (Genesis 2:19). Today's parents teach their children to identify horses, chickens, cows, dogs, and cats and rejoice when their toddlers repeat the words back to them, even if comically garbled. When God created Adam, He must have created him not only with the ability to speak but also with the vocabulary and the capacity to decide, based on his observations, what each animal should be named.

But there was a deeper reason for creating Adam first and asking him to name all the animals. After reviewing the animal pairs, he quickly realized that "none of these was the right kind of partner" for him (verse 19, CEV). Ellen White explains that "man was not made to dwell in solitude; he was to be a social being. Without companionship the beautiful scenes and delightful employments of Eden would have failed to yield perfect happiness. Even communion with angels could not have satisfied his desire for sympathy and companionship. There was none of the same nature to love and to be loved."[2] Once Adam came to that realization, it was the right time for God to perform skilled surgery and create a compatible mate for him. God created them, brought them together, and performed the first wedding ceremony.³

No, it is not good that people should be alone! Though everyone will go through a season when they have no marriage companion, they need not be alone. Human beings were created for social interaction, and it is in relationships that they grow and thrive best.

The downside of love

"I am not able to bear all these people alone, because the burden is too heavy for me" (Numbers 11:14). This lament from Moses was the result of leading the Israelite slaves from Egypt into a land of freedom. While he had Aaron, Miriam, his wife, and others around him, he felt alone in this responsibility.

Jesus must have felt this way too. Not only was He unmarried, even those closest to Him disappeared in His time of need. While He struggled in Gethsemane, they slept when He needed their prayers and their presence the most (Matthew 26:36–46).

The season of being alone is tough because there is no one to warm us up when we are cold, no one to help us fight aggressors, and no one to lift us up when we are down. Ecclesiastes 4 speaks of the benefits of two rather than one, but at the end of verse 12, the writer introduces an additional idea: "A threefold cord is not quickly broken." In a marital relationship, that third person (or rather First Person) is God. For the unmarried, that other person must also be God: "He Himself has said, 'I will never leave you nor forsake you' " (Hebrews 13:5). At the same time, we need to remember that those words in Hebrews are preceded by these: "Be content with such things as you have."

Look around your Sabbath School class or scan the church pews during church. How many people do not have anyone sitting by them? How many are unmarried? In practical terms, what can you do to help your church members feel less alone?

Seasons of Being Alone

Numerous people in our churches are not married and find their primary source of companionship among fellow believers. But many of them arrive at church and leave without being greeted; no one chooses to sit by them, and no one invites them home. The widow or widower sits alone. The person whose spouse is not a member of the church attends services by himself or herself while also feeling alienated at home. The divorced person, embarrassed, ashamed, or perhaps relieved, avoids the judging eyes of the saints, hoping for an encouraging word, an understanding heart, or the warm touch of someone's hand.

The upside of being alone

The seasons of being alone are troubling but, in some cases, not all bad. Though they too need people in their lives, introverts can be content to be alone for periods of time, happy for the opportunity to recharge their emotional batteries. Additionally, a single person may find it easier to move from place to place, volunteer on short-term mission projects, or perhaps move permanently to the mission field without having to consider a spouse's employment or their children's education. Think for a moment. How would being single impact your life and mission for Christ?

While we read about the crowds that surrounded Jesus and of His constant companions, He, too, needed alone time.

> The Saviour loved the solitude of the mountain in which to hold communion with His Father. Through the day He labored earnestly to save men from destruction. He healed the sick, comforted the mourning, called the dead to life, and brought hope and cheer to the despairing. After His work for the day was finished, He went forth, evening after evening, away from the confusion of the city, and bowed in prayer to His Father. Frequently He continued His petitions through the entire night; but He came from these seasons of communion invigorated and refreshed, braced for duty and for trial.[4]

Family Seasons

A time to break up

In his book of wisdom, King Solomon tells us that there is "a time to kill, and a time to heal; a time to break down, and a time to build up" (Ecclesiastes 3:3, ESV). There may come a time in the life of an unmarried person when he or she needs to end a bad or potentially harmful relationship. Many single people, anxious to get married, find themselves in toxic relationships. They think if they try hard enough, give in enough, change enough, things will improve. They hope life will be different once they get married. In reality, if there are red flags before the wedding day, they should evaluate the condition of their relationship and perhaps even end it before it is too late. Some couples even tolerate abuse before they are married—abuse that is destined to worsen after the marriage is consummated.

When people are in abusive relationships, asking why they do not leave does not offer much help. They may be economically dependent on the abuser. Their culture may frown on a breakup. The church may inadvertently encourage such terrible treatment by telling abused people that they must forgive their abuser or that they must submit to them as a loving spouse should. Instead, we can remind them that God's plan for marriage is that a husband and wife should love, respect, and care for each other. We can assure them that God has something better for them: "For I know the thoughts that I think toward you, says the LORD, thoughts of peace and not of evil, to give you a future and a hope" (Jeremiah 29:11).

The season of being alone may not be easy, but it is better than being in an abusive relationship. Our younger daughter once wisely told us, "I'd rather be alone and single than alone and married."

When a relationship ends

" 'Til death do us part" is a phrase often repeated by a couple at the end of their marriage vows. The Bible does not tell us whether Adam or Eve died first, but it must have been particularly painful for the one left behind. "As they witnessed in drooping flower and falling leaf the first signs of decay, Adam and his companion mourned more deeply than men now mourn over their dead."[5] Imagine what it must have been like for Adam or Eve to witness the death of the other after hundreds of years together. What remorse for their poor decision in Eden! Sadly, the one who remained could only blame himself or herself.

Today death is nothing new. We live with it at every turn, but losing a spouse after decades of marriage is especially difficult. Like death, divorce is traumatic and painful for both the couple and their children. If in marriage two become one, then dividing that one is something like an amputation. It may be necessary, but it will leave scars that affect each party for the rest of their lives.

The New Living Translation renders Malachi 2:16 in a heart-wrenching way: " 'For I hate divorce!' says the Lord, the God of Israel. 'To divorce your wife is to overwhelm her with cruelty,' says the Lord of Heaven's Armies. 'So guard your heart; do not be unfaithful to your wife.' " The pain lingers after divorce, particularly if the couple has children as they will likely see each other again and again as they attend graduations, weddings, and milestone events.

People suffering through a collapsing marriage will experience various emotions. Probably the first and most common feeling is grief. Depending on the individual, it may last from several months to several years with varying intensity. Some may experience fear—fear of the unknown, fear of financial difficulties, and/or fear of being unable to cope. Some may go through periods of depression, anger, and loneliness.

When a marriage ends through death or divorce, a time of reflection should follow. It can be a special season of remembrance of all that was enjoyed together. It can be a time of healing and planning. The grieving person can ask himself or herself, *How can I make this experience as positive as possible?*

It is particularly important to keep the well-being of children in mind. Make them a top priority. Parents should avoid using them against the former spouse or saying negative things to the children about the other parent. Instead, parents should encourage a healthy relationship with the other parent and ask themselves, What is best for the children? No matter the cause of the divorce, parents should cooperate with each other for the benefit of their children.

Spiritually single
In church life, we meet people who are married but attend alone or only with their children. Their spouse may be of a different faith or may have stopped practicing the faith. Perhaps one spouse joined the church, and the other did not. For these reasons and more, these members come to church alone. They attend fellowship dinners alone. They attend socials alone. They are often unable to contribute financially to the church's ministry because their spouse is unsupportive. Job was "blameless and upright, and one who feared God and shunned evil" (Job 1:1), but it appears his wife did not share his experience (Job 2:9). In the Bible, we find encouraging words for those who do not have a spiritual companion by their side: "For your Maker is your husband, the LORD of hosts is His name; and your Redeemer is the Holy One of Israel" (Isaiah 54:5; see also Hosea 2:19, 20; Psalm 72:12). Those married to an unbelieving spouse should hold on to God's promises:

- "Leave your fatherless children, I will preserve them alive; and let your widows trust in Me" (Jeremiah 49:11).
- "The LORD watches over the strangers; He relieves the fatherless and widow" (Psalm 146:9).
- "A father of the fatherless, a defender of widows, is God in His holy habitation" (Psalm 68:5).

While all of these promises are encouraging and trustworthy, those who are spiritually single also need the love, help, and compassion of the church family. The church is, and should be, a loving and embracing place for everyone. For someone who does not have a spiritual companion, parenting can be particularly challenging. Solomon admonishes parents to "train up a child in the way he should go" and to not "withhold good from those to whom it is due, when it is in the power of your hand to do so," and this includes correction (Proverbs 22:6; 3:27; 23:13). The apostle Paul adds that children should be taught to honor and obey their parents (Ephesians 6:1, 2). And parents, especially fathers, ought not to provoke their children to anger (see verse 4).

Raising children is a challenge for two parents and even more so for single parents. The church family can be a helpful resource in this situation. Paul suggests that a healthy church family needs a mentoring program where the older men and women teach the younger ones (Titus 2). James aptly describes this kind of church: "Pure and undefiled religion before God and the Father is this: to visit orphans and widows in their trouble" (James 1:27).

For further consideration

1. While we cannot change our circumstances, what steps can we take to turn the downside of the single life into an upside? If connections start with you, what can you do to connect with others in the church and in your community?

2. What do you think Paul meant when he wrote, "In every church I tell the people to stay as they were when the Lord Jesus chose them and God called them to be his own. Now I say the same thing to you" (1 Corinthians 7:17, CEV)?

3. Chances are that there are people around you, even in church, who are being abused by someone close to them. What kind of assistance could you provide in helping them to stop accepting abuse as normal? What practical advice could you give? (Ephesians 5:28; Psalms 20:1, 2; 121:1, 2.)

4. God values us in three important ways: our identity, our significance, and our purpose in Christ. Which of the following verses apply to each of these? Matthew 28:19, 20; John 10:10;

15:14; Ephesians 2:10; 1 Peter 2:10; 1 John 3:1.

---

1. Ellen G. White, *Patriarchs and Prophets* (Mountain View, CA: Pacific Press®, 1958), 46.
2. White, *Patriarchs and Prophets*, 46.
3. White, *Patriarchs and Prophets*, 46.
4. Ellen G. White, *Gospel Workers* (Washington, DC: Review and Herald®, 1915), 256.
5. White, *Patriarchs and Prophets*, 62.

CHAPTER 5

Seasons of Wisdom

All living organisms experience growth, and farmers understand the growth cycle better than most. First, a field is prepared and tilled. Soon after, seeds are placed in the earth and spaced so that each sprouting plant will receive the nutrients it needs without being crowded by other plants. The newly planted seeds are then watered and finally, the harvest arrives, and the growth cycle is complete. The process of preparation, planting, and harvesting will be repeated during the next planting season.

Just like the plant kingdom, animals and humans experience a predictable cycle of growth. It begins with the fertilization of the egg, proceeds to cell division that forms the embryo, and continues to the development of the fetus. A newborn baby continues the cycle of growth from childhood to adulthood—and from birth to death. Sometimes, however, the cycle's predictable pattern experiences problems, and a child will be born with special needs, a terminal illness, or some other disease. Later, accidents happen, life changes, and the "predictable" cycle suddenly becomes unreliable.

The seasons of growth merge into one another and form part of our life cycle. We study, we learn, and we follow the example of others. Hopefully, we go on to be helpful teachers and leaders.

Family Seasons

From a spiritual point of view, our advancement toward eternity begins with the new-birth experience and continues with our daily growth in Jesus. While development is individual, it affects those around us. As people grow and change, families and churches cannot help but follow suit. Growth is part of God's plan, even throughout eternity.

Even Jesus, the perfect Song of God, did not arrive on earth all grown up. The Bible describes Jesus' growth quite simply: "And Jesus grew in wisdom and stature, and in favor with God and man" (Luke 2:52, NIV). When He was twelve years old, He was already teaching and questioning formally trained rabbis, and those who heard Him were "surprised at how much he knew and at the answers he gave" (verse 47, CEV). His growth was harmonious in every area of life.

Through education and experience, we should also be growing in knowledge and wisdom. Solomon, the wisest man who ever lived, compiled wise sayings, questions, poems, and instructions into the book of Proverbs. He repeatedly highlights the value of wisdom, mentioning it more than fifty times:

- "God blesses everyone who has wisdom and common sense" (Proverbs 3:13, CEV).
- "The best thing about Wisdom is Wisdom herself; good sense is more important than anything else" (Proverbs 4:7, CEV).
- "Wisdom is a life-giving tree, the source of happiness for all who hold on to her" (Proverbs 3:18, CEV).
- "Wisdom is worth much more than precious jewels or anything else you desire" (Proverbs 8:11, CEV).

Along with Solomon and with the psalmist, we can ask God, "Give me wisdom and good sense" (2 Chronicles 1:10; Psalm 119:66, CEV).

Unfortunately, not all people choose to grow in wisdom. Twice in the book of Psalms we read of the fool who says in his heart that there is no God (Psalms 14:1; 53:1). In the New Testament, half the virgins in Jesus' parable of the ten virgins were foolish (Matthew 25:1–13); and Paul refers to those who did not acknowledge God as "foolish, faithless, heartless, ruthless" (Romans 1:31, NRSV).

Love the right woman

A wise man will carefully consider the woman he marries. One of the most extensive and best-known biblical depictions of a godly woman is found in Proverbs 31:10–31. Authored by King Lemuel, these twenty-two verses are written in the form of a beautiful acrostic following the pattern of the twenty-two letters of the Hebrew alphabet.

This virtuous woman—literally a woman of power—is strong, energetic, and possesses excellent qualities. The original Hebrew suggests she is a woman of firm character. Up to this point,

> the book of Proverbs has been devoted to inculcating the ideal of a wise man. It now concludes with a poem describing a wise woman, praising her energy, her economic talents, and her personal virtues. This is not one specific woman but an ideal, a paragon of female virtues. These virtues are essentially shared by the ideal man described elsewhere. . . . Contrary to a common notion of woman's status in the ancient world, this woman has considerable independence in interacting with outsiders and conducting business, even in acquiring real estate. This allows her husband to spend his time sitting in the city gates, presumably conducting civic business and serving as a judge. . . . The poem is traditionally recited by Jewish men to their wives on Sabbath evening, before the Kiddush (the sanctification of the Sabbath over wine). It is also often recited at funerals of women.[1]

While some men may look for a woman who literally meets all the detailed descriptions of this virtuous woman, they may be better off seeking how they can become virtuous men. In the small, delightful book *Letters to Young Lovers*, Ellen White gives practical advice for choosing a future mate. To young men, she writes, "Let a young man seek one to stand by his side who is fitted to bear her share of life's burdens, one whose influence will ennoble and refine him, and who will make him happy in her love."[2] She adds several Bible texts as an example of what he should be looking for:

> "A prudent wife is from the Lord." "The heart of her husband doth safely trust in her." "She will do him good and not evil all the days of her life." "She openeth her mouth with wisdom; and in her tongue is the law of kindness. She looketh well to the ways of her household, and eateth not the bread of idleness. Her children arise up, and call her blessed; her husband also, and he praiseth her. Many daughters have done virtuously, but thou excellest them all." "Whoso findeth a wife findeth a good thing, and obtaineth favour of the Lord." Proverbs 19:14; 31:11, 12, 26-29; 18:22.[3]

Mrs. White balances her advice to young men by addressing young ladies:

> Before giving her hand in marriage, every woman should inquire whether he with whom she is about to unite her destiny is worthy. What has been his past record? Is his life pure? Is the love which he expresses of a noble, elevated character, or is it a mere emotional fondness? Has he the traits of character that will make her happy? Can she find true peace and joy in his affection? Will she be allowed to preserve her individuality, or must her judgment and conscience be surrendered to the control of her husband? As a disciple of Christ, she is not her own; she has been bought with a price. Can she honor the Saviour's claims as supreme? Will body and soul, thoughts and

purposes, be preserved pure and holy? These questions have a vital bearing upon the well-being of every woman who enters the marriage relation.

Let the questions be raised, Will this union help me heavenward? will it increase my love for God? and will it enlarge my sphere of usefulness in this life? If these reflections present no drawback, then in the fear of God move forward.[4]

A call to fathers

We have been asked on many occasions, "What is the best gift parents can give their children?" We submit that the answer to that question is your marriage to your spouse. Some people have disagreed, telling us the best gift we can give our children is a faith, knowledge, and love for God. We agree with that assessment; however, we also assert that it is in the home where children first learn to develop faith, knowledge, and love for God. Many children have a difficult time believing in a God that was not able to keep their parents together and their home intact. "It is in the home that the education of the child is to begin. Here is his first school. Here, with his parents as instructors, he is to learn the lessons that are to guide him throughout life—lessons of respect, obedience, reverence, self-control."[5] Ellen White also writes, "The family circle is the school in which the child receives its first and most enduring lessons. Hence parents should be much at home. By precept and example, they should teach their children the love and the fear of God; teach them to be intelligent, social, affectionate, to cultivate habits of industry, economy, and self-denial. By giving their children love, sympathy, and encouragement at home, parents may provide for them a safe and welcome retreat from many of the world's temptations."[6]

If you want to give your children the best gift—something that will prepare them for a successful life in this world and for eternity in the earth made new—strengthen your relationship with your spouse.

Correction with love

When it comes to your children, practice wise and beneficial discipline. At the same time, provide consistent and fair guidance. Paul wrote to the church in Thessalonica and described three ways in which this is accomplished: (1) by exhorting, which means to urge, advise, and earnestly caution; (2) by comforting, which means to soothe, console, and cheer; and (3) by charging your child, which means to issue a command or instruction or to hold the child accountable for an action (1 Thessalonians 2:11, 12).

As parents, we need to remember that each child is as unique, different, and beautiful as an individual snowflake. Anyone who has more than one child knows about the differences in learning styles and behavior. Some children can be disciplined with a stern look; others fail to respond to the sharpest reprimand. Effective child training requires parents to customize their approach to the temperament of the individual child.

What is of concern to us is when parents take the words of Proverbs and "beat" their children into submission. God, our loving Parent, does not abuse His children any more than He wants us to abuse ours. Perhaps it would be good to remember what constitutes abusive behavior:

- Any physical punishment that is harsh and unreasonably painful, even though it may result in changed behavior.
- Any impulsive, irrational punishment that is inflicted merely as an appeasement for parental anger.
- Any treatment of children that makes them feel embarrassed or belittled, whether it is in public or private.
- Any words that cut down children's self-respect or diminishes the positive feelings they have about themselves.
- Any behavior that causes children to feel alienated from their family or from God.

It is important to understand the difference between

punishment and discipline. *Punishment* is a penalty imposed upon a child for doing something wrong. Punishment involves the experience of pain, loss, or suffering for a wrong. At times, parents or caregivers punish the child with the intent to hurt, physically or emotionally, so that the child will learn that wrongdoing is painful and thus choose, or be forced to choose, what is right. On other occasions, parents or caregivers punish from a mistaken sense of justice that demands children must pay a penalty for their "crimes" or wrongdoing.

Discipline, on the other hand, is a teaching process. It leads to the prevention or the resolution of conflict. Discipline helps children improve themselves. It helps them learn lessons that will make them better people. The primary aim of discipline is to resolve impending conflict and teach children self-discipline. Remember that the words *discipline* and *disciple* come from the same root word. The goal of parenting is to make disciples, teaching children by word and example to become followers of Jesus. Punishment will not help parents achieve this objective.

The humor of Proverbs

The book of Proverbs is a collection of wise sayings that occasionally carry a message tinged with humor. Solomon understood that "happiness makes you smile; sorrow can crush you" (Proverbs 15:13, CEV); "A cheerful heart is good medicine, but a broken spirit saps a person's strength" (Proverbs 17:22, NLT). *Proverbs* are simple, concrete sayings that are popularly known and often repeated. They are usually metaphorical and characterized by nuggets of truth, based on common sense and experience. Some proverbs are even humorous:

1. A man in love mistakes a pimple for a dimple.
2. The lion that stays at home too long will start to feel like a cat.
3. He who asks questions is a fool for a minute, he who does not, remains a fool forever.

Family Seasons

4. If you understand everything, you must be misinformed.
5. If you can't convince them, confuse them.[7]

Solomon must have had a healthy sense of humor as he included some very interesting proverbs in his book. Here is a small sample that sound funny but which are loaded with truth:

> A beautiful woman
>   who acts foolishly
>   is like a gold ring
>   on the snout of a pig (Proverbs 11:22, CEV).

"As charcoal is to burning coals, and wood to fire, so is a contentious man to kindle strife" (Proverbs 26:21).

For wives who think they can nag their husbands into doing what they ask, Solomon reminds them that

> it's better to stay outside
>   on the roof of your house
>   than to live inside
>   with a nagging wife. . . .
>
> It's better out in the desert
>   than at home with a nagging,
>   complaining wife (Proverbs 21:9, 19, CEV).

The peace of home is a blessing we all long for. Solomon provides an illustration when we do not enjoy such a haven:

> A dry crust of bread eaten
>   in peace and quiet
>   is better than a feast eaten
>   where everyone argues (Proverbs 17:1, CEV).

Families would do well to spend time studying and practicing these wise proverbs. They will enrich your household and make your heart glad.

For further consideration

1. Using a concordance, make a list of proverbs that apply to different members of the family. What modern application can you make of each?

2. Proverbs 31 lists several qualities of a virtuous woman. Using Bible texts make a comparable list for the qualities of a virtuous man.

---

1. A. Berlin, M. Z. Brettler, and M. Fishbane, eds., *The Jewish Study Bible* (New York: Oxford University Press, 2004), 1497.

2. Ellen. G. White, *Letters to Young Lovers* (Mountain View, CA: Pacific Press®, 1983), 20.

3. White, *Letters to Young Lovers*, 20.

4. White, *Letters to Young Lovers*, 23.

5. Ellen G. White, *The Adventist Home* (Washington, DC: Review and Herald®, 1952), 182.

6. Ellen G. White, *Fundamentals of Christian Education* (Nashville, TN: Southern Pub. Assn., 1923), 65.

7. Danicaparra, June 19, 2016, comment on Kenreycesar, "Give 5 Example of Humorous Proverbs," Brainly, June 19, 2016, https://brainly.ph/question/315898.

CHAPTER 6

Seasons of Marriage

"At a wedding the groom is the one who gets married. The best man is glad just to be there and to hear the groom's voice" (John 3:29, CEV). So much has changed since biblical times, particularly the practice of parents choosing a wife for their son. But parents in many Eastern cultures still arrange their children's marriages. In some places, a man wishing to marry a certain young lady is required to present her parents with a bride price of money, farm animals, or some other tangible form of payment. The more valuable the young lady and the better off the groom, the higher the price.

Of course, Western cultures approach courtship quite differently: couples meet, get acquainted, become engaged, marry, and form their own homes. And with technology playing an increasingly important role in our culture, some singles look for a date, and possible spouse, on the internet or a phone app. Unfortunately, it seems as if this abundance of connectivity is isolating us more than ever, even as it provides us with numerous opportunities to meet and interact with people all over the world. What can the Bible possibly teach modern people about relationships? As it turns out, quite a bit. The small, almost inconspicuous Old Testament book of the Song of Solomon offers an amazing glimpse into God's plan for marriage.

Family Seasons

Before the wedding

Before reading this section, read Song of Solomon 1:1–3:5. Song of Solomon begins with the young Shulamite woman fantasizing about her beloved and what it will be like when they are married: "O that you would kiss me" (Song of Solomon 1:2, RSV). "O that his left hand were under my head, and that his right hand embraced me!" (Song of Solomon 2:6, RSV). While many Bible versions render these verses as an invitation or an order ("Let him kiss me" [Song of Solomon 1:2, KJV], "Kiss me" [Song of Solomon 1:2, NLT]), the Revised Standard Version portrays them as the fantasies of a young woman as she contemplates marriage to her beloved.

We do not have to wait long to learn what this Shulamite woman desires from her man: the kisses of his mouth. These kisses are more intimate than the familial kisses a brother and sister may exchange (Song of Solomon 8:1). She also desires to be caressed—a physical intimacy that is passionate and not simply a desire for procreation. Her desire for him is compared to tasting sweet wine (Song of Solomon 1:2), which, like true love, leaves a person with a desire for more.

From touch and taste, the young woman's imagination moves to her sense of smell as she enjoys the fragrance of his anointing oils (verse 3). But it is not just the physical attributes that draw her, she is also attracted to his character when she says, "Your name is oil poured out" (verse 3, RSV). A person's name represented his character or reputation and comparing her groom's name to perfume meant that his character was pleasing and attractive to her (2 Samuel 7:9). In fact, that is the reason why she says many are attracted to him.

While this dreamy young woman longs for the day she will be held in the embrace of her husband, she is careful to share with her unmarried friends' practical advice. Three times she tells them "not to awaken love until the time is right" (Song of Solomon 2:7; 3:5; 8:4, NLT). Eugene Peterson's paraphrased Bible renders her admonition, "Don't excite love, don't stir it up, until the time is ripe—

and you're ready" (Song of Solomon 2:7; 3:5; 8:4, *The Message*).

The Shulamite is a modest and humble young woman who seeks the assurance that her suitor finds her attractive (Song of Solomon 1:5, 6, RSV). To reassure her, the beloved compares her to a mare (verse 9), not the most flattering comparison for our ears today, but one that underscored the beauty and attractiveness he found in her (verse 15). He adds that she is "a lily among thorns" (Song of Solomon 2:2), to which she responds that he is like "an apple tree among the trees of the woods" (Song of Solomon 2:3). She also compares him to a "gazelle or a young stag" (verse 9). From this exchange, we can learn that complimenting your spouse regularly validates him or her, giving your spouse needed value and encouragement.

At this stage, the Shulamite and her beloved are not married, but they know it is time for them to join their lives together (Song of Solomon 3:4, 5). She longs to be with him: "Upon my bed by night I sought him whom my soul loves; I sought him, but found him not" (verse 1, RSV).

The wedding

Before reading this section, read Song of Solomon 3:6–4:7. In Jesus' parable of the ten virgins, the bridegroom was delayed. "At midnight a cry was heard: 'Behold, the bridegroom is coming; go out to meet him!' " (Matthew 25:6). In the Song of Solomon, the young bride also speaks of an arriving bridegroom. With shouts of excitement, she asks,

> Who is this coming out of the wilderness
> Like pillars of smoke,
> Perfumed with myrrh and frankincense,
> With all the merchant's fragrant powders? (Song of Solomon 3:6).

It is Solomon her beloved, attired in the finest of royal garments.

Family Seasons

As a popular saying goes, "There's no such thing as an ugly bride." If we go by Solomon's detailed description of his beloved, she was particularly beautiful. He begins at her eyes, probably the most personal and expressive of her features, and compares them to doves, shy and inaccessible when they hide in the clefts of a rock (Song of Solomon 4:1; cf. 2:14). Her hair, like a flock of goats, evokes the image of motion and life (Song of Solomon 4:1). Her teeth, perfectly white and symmetrical, are a sign of health (verse 2). From the blackness of her eyes and hair to the whiteness of her teeth, Solomon now focuses on the redness of her lips and temples; like "a strand of scarlet" and like a pomegranate respectively (verse 3). Her neck, "like the tower of David," gives us the image of strength and confidence (verse 4). Just as her teeth each have a twin, so her breasts are twins, denoting symmetry as well as fertility (verse 5).

It should be noted that while the beloved's account of his bride has often been described as erotic, he has spent most of his time describing her face. It is also of interest that Solomon points out seven features of particular note: her eyes, hair, teeth, lips or mouth, temples, neck, and breasts. The number seven denotes perfection, and Solomon describes his bride as the perfect woman for him. No wonder he says, "My darling, you are lovely in every way" (verse 7, CEV). As soon as the wedding takes place, Solomon calls his bride not just "my love" but also "my spouse" (verses 1, 7, 8).

The marriage is consummated

Before reading this section, read Song of Solomon 4:8–5:1. The midpoint in the Song of Solomon comes at 4:16–5:1. Interestingly, exactly 111 lines of Hebrew poetry precede Song of Solomon 4:16, and 111 lines of Hebrew poetry follows Song of Solomon 5:1.[1] These verses describe the consummation of the marriage between Solomon and the Shulamite. It is vital to understand what is taking place here. As Solomon looks on his new bride, he says of her,

> My bride, my very own,
> you are a garden,
> a fountain
> > closed off to all others (Song of Solomon 4:12, CEV).

During many wedding ceremonies, the couples repeat the vows that ask, "Do you promise to love, honor, cherish, and protect him/her, forsaking all others and holding only to him/her forevermore?" In similar manner, Solomon declares of his bride that she is closed off to all others. She is his and only his. His bride now offers an invitation: "Let my beloved come into his garden" (verse 16, KJV), and they lovingly consummate their marriage to each other. Once consummated ("I have come to my garden" [Song of Solomon 5:1]), he rejoices in the sweetness of marital love and intimacy and calls her his spouse.

While this intimate description of marital love is delightful in its simplicity and beauty, it is important to notice a conversation between the bride and her brothers that evidently took place before the wedding. While still a young, unmarried lady, they say of her,

> We have a little sister
> > too young to have breasts.
> What will we do for our sister
> > if someone asks to marry her? (Song of Solomon 8:8, NLT).

The brothers talk about her sexual activity, wondering,

> If she is a virgin, like a wall,
> > we will protect her with a silver tower.
> But if she is promiscuous, like a swinging door,
> > we will block her door with a cedar bar (verse 9, NLT).

With confidence, she assures them, "I am a wall, and my breasts like the towers thereof then was I in his eyes as one that found peace" (verse 10, ASV). She has nothing to be ashamed of as she gives her husband what no other has had or can have.

This message in the Song of Solomon—the bride's call to not awaken love until the right time—is a message young people still need to hear. The bride proudly proclaimed to her brothers that she was a wall, a sealed garden, a fountain enclosed, reserved for her beloved.

Distance and conflict

Before reading this section, read Song of Solomon 5:2–6:3. The love story of the Song of Solomon could have ended with the groom encouraging his friends to celebrate his marriage—"Eat, O friends! Drink, yes, drink deeply, O beloved ones!" (Song of Solomon 5:1). If it were a fairy tale, it would have ended with the words *and they lived happily ever after*. But anyone who has been married for some time knows that marriage is not always a bed of roses. When two selfish people with different backgrounds, personalities, habits, and idiosyncrasies bring their idealistic expectations to marriage, conflict is unavoidable. Unfortunately, conflict often leads to distance, particularly in the bedroom, and some couples use marital intimacy as ransom for their selfish desires.

The husband and wife of Song of Solomon enact a scene repeated in many homes. In chapter 2, the man invites the woman to come away with him, outside the house (verses 10, 13). It is his marriage proposal of sorts. Now that they are married, he is not inviting her to come out but rather he wants to come into his house (Song of Solomon 5:2). There is an evident shift in their marital status. The intent of his request is sexual in nature, and he uses kind, gentle, loving words toward his wife to encourage her to accept his invitation: "Open for me, my sister, my love, my dove, my perfect one" (verse 2). But she rejects him with an excuse:

I have taken off my robe;

> How can I put it on again?
> I have washed my feet;
> How can I defile them? (verse 3).

When she finally agrees to his advances, he is not there anymore (verses 4–6). Often couples play this power game, which only leads to dissatisfaction with each other and the marriage.

While there may be times when marriage partners do not have sexual relations, the apostle Paul provides four principles that couples should consider when abstaining from sex: "Do not deprive one another except [1] with [mutual] consent [2] for a time, [3] that you may give yourselves to fasting and prayer; and [4] come together again so that Satan does not tempt you because of your lack of self-control" (1 Corinthians 7:5). Fortunately, by Song of Solomon 6:2, the couple has resumed their intimacy and continued to strengthen their marital bond (verses 2, 3).

A lifetime commitment

Before reading this section, read Song of Solomon 6:4–8:14. With the words "I am my beloved's, and my beloved is mine," the Shulamite tells us that she and her beloved have been reconciled (Song of Solomon 6:3). The distance between them is closed, and they come together again (verses 11, 12). This roller coaster of conflict and peace is inevitable in marriage as the stresses of life pull couples in different directions. Enjoying resolution and finding satisfaction in a relationship is like running in green pastures, marveling at the blossoms of the valley, and eating fresh, vine-ripened fruit (verse 11).

There is an important truth worth noting in this section of the book. Compare the earlier description of the Shulamite's beloved and his latest description of her (Song of Solomon 5:10–16; 6:4–10; 7:1–9). Notice the attributes each sees in the other. When the Shulamite talks about her husband, she uses the language of strength, courage, and power: "His hands are rods of gold" (Song of Solomon 5:14); "his legs are pillars of marble set on bases of fine gold" (verse 15); and "his body is carved ivory" (verse 14). But even though he epitomizes strength, he speaks kindly and lovingly to her; indeed, he is her friend (verse 16).

As he writes about her in Song of Solomon 4, he describes only what he can see, from her hair down to her breasts; the rest of her body is hidden from his eyes. He has respected her and has not seen or tried to see what only a husband should. In chapter 7, after they have become husband and wife, he gives a more detailed description of her body, now that it is unveiled for him. In chapter 4, he lists seven features of her upper body and declares her to be perfect. Here in chapter 7, he lists twelve physical attributes to denote how complete she is—she lacks nothing. There is no one that compares to her (Song of Solomon 6:8, 9). In their mutual love, they complete each other.

But a lasting relationship cannot be based on outward beauty alone. Our bodies age, and no amount of diet, exercise, or plastic surgery will keep us looking young forever. An important dynamic of Solomon and the Shulamite's marriage is a lifelong, committed relationship. Three times they affirm they belong to each other (Song of Solomon 2:16; 6:3; 7:10). The first time it is a recognition of mutual ownership (cf. Ephesians 5:21, 33). The second time the woman reverses the order of ownership in affirmation of her submission (cf. verses 22, 23). The third time the man expresses his desire for her (cf. verses 24–32). This appears to be a theme in Scripture: the message of mutual submission in marriage. This submission is clearly taught in Ephesians 5:21 and is also found in the Song of Solomon. Love like this is like a seal that cannot be broken, and it cannot be drowned (Song of Solomon 8:6, 7).

> God has ordained that there should be perfect love and harmony between those who enter into the marriage relation. Let bride and bridegroom, in the presence of the heavenly universe, pledge themselves to love each other as God has ordained they should. . . . The wife is to respect

and reverence her husband, and the husband is to love and cherish his wife.

Men and women, at the beginning of married life, should reconsecrate themselves to God.[2]

For further consideration

1. Solomon describes his wife as perfect (Song of Solomon 4:1–5; 6:9; 7:1–9). Compare this description with Adam's expression when he first saw Eve (Genesis 2:23, CEV). How does this inform a husband's relationship with his wife? (See Ephesians 5:28, 29.)

2. Read Proverbs 31:26 and Proverbs 25:11. How important are our words? What is their role in tearing down or building up our spouse and weakening or strengthening our marriage? For further reading on the power of words, see James 1:26; 3:5–11; 1 John 3:18.

---

1. *Andrews Study Bible* (Berrien Springs, MI: Andrews University Press, 2010), note on Song of Solomon 4:16–5:1.

2. Ellen G. White, *The Adventist Home* (Washington, DC: Review and Herald®, 1952), 103.

CHAPTER 17

Seasons of Unity

The opening line of *Anna Karenina*, Leo Tolstoy's classic book, states an interesting truth: "All happy families resemble one another; every unhappy family is unhappy in its own way."[1] We have heard it said that if you think you know a perfect family, you do not know the family very well! Every family, no matter how good, healthy, or loving, has periodic challenges in establishing and maintaining love and unity.

One of the first obvious results of Adam and Eve's fall was the breakup of the oneness and intimacy they had previously enjoyed. Ellen White states, "The cause of division and discord in families and in the church is separation from Christ. To come near to Christ is to come near to one another. The secret of true unity in the church and in the family is not diplomacy, not management, not a superhuman effort to overcome difficulties—though there will be much of this to do—but union with Christ."[2]

Christ the center

We all long for unity in the family. The psalmist declares, "It is truly wonderful when relatives live together in peace" (Psalm 133:1, CEV). But unity in any organization cannot be forced, imposed, or legislated. "The secret of unity is found in the equality of believers in Christ. The reason for all division, discord, and difference is found in separation from Christ. Christ is the center to which all should be attracted; for the nearer we approach the center, the closer we shall come together in feeling, in sympathy, in love, growing into the character and image of Jesus. With God there is no respect of persons."[3]

When we as a family pull together with Jesus at the center, we cannot help but be drawn to Him and each other. We are told how to treat one another twenty-five times in the New Testament. Among the admonitions, we are told to love one another (1 Thessalonians 3:12), accept one another (Romans 15:7), have the same care for one another as we have for ourselves (Mark 12:31), submit to one another (Ephesians 5:21), edify one another (Ephesians 4:29), and serve one another in love (Galatians 5:13).

Selfishness: Family destroyer

The moment Adam and Eve ate of the forbidden fruit, they stopped looking to bless each other and, instead, focused on self-protection. When God asked them what they had done, Adam pointed an accusatory finger at his wife. Eve, in turn, pointed to the serpent and indirectly at God who had created it. Since that moment, every marriage has consisted of two broken individuals who are trying to figure out how to be in fellowship together. Though we have an idea of how things should go, we are often frustrated by disappointing results.

Selfishness is the attitude of being concerned with one's own interests above the interests of others. The antidote for selfishness is to "do nothing from selfishness or empty conceit, but with humility of mind regard one another as more important than yourselves; do not merely look out for your own personal interests, but also for the interests of others" (Philippians 2:3, 4, NASB).

Submission

According to 1 Kings 14:21, Rehoboam, King Solomon's son, was forty-one years old when he became king of Israel. Sadly, he had not learned the lesson of servant leadership. As soon as he was installed as king in Shechem, many of the leaders of the country approached him with a request to lift the heavy yoke of taxation and forced labor that his father had imposed. When he consulted with the elders who had advised his father, they told him, "If today you will be a servant to these people and serve them and give them a favorable answer, they will always be your servants" (1 Kings 12:7, NIV). But Rehoboam did not listen. Instead, he followed the counsel of the friends with whom he had grown up. He threatened the people and promised even harsher treatment than his father had given them. Because he did not learn to serve downward, he lost ten of the twelve tribes from his kingdom, which created an irreparable chasm among the nation of God's people.

Fortunately, the Bible leaves us with more than Rehoboam's example of how not to treat people. In the New Testament, we discover Jesus and the true nature of submission. At His last Passover meal, after three and a half years of ministry, He knew His life would soon come to an end. In a matter of hours, He would be arrested, tried illegally, condemned to die, and would suffer the cruelest of deaths. He had invested nearly forty-two months of His thirty-three years to prepare His disciples for this moment and for eternity. He showed them, through word and act, what their loving heavenly Father was like. He healed the sick, raised the dead, and taught like no one ever had. Now, in their last few minutes together, what would Jesus tell His disciples? What would He do to impress them one last time?

This meeting did not take place in a public setting but rather in the privacy of a home, during what is traditionally a family celebration. Among other things, Jesus tells His disciples that though He will be leaving, He will return for them. In the meantime, they will have another Friend, just like Him, to guide and teach them. But He also gave them one final important lesson: "If you want to be first, you must be the slave of the rest" (Matthew 20:27, CEV).

Although Jesus' entire life was one of service to others, the most notable example of His servanthood was that of washing His disciples' feet (John 13:1–17). This mundane act of service left a profound impression on His followers. It was not in spite of His greatness but rather because of it that Jesus served His disciples that evening. Through His own attitude toward servanthood, He taught humanity that true greatness in the kingdom of God consists not in position or authority but in serving one another. Jesus "made Himself of no reputation, taking the form of a bondservant" (Philippians 2:7).

Jesus recognized that the common belief and practice in the world is that the lesser serves the greater (Luke 22:27). And though this may be true in the world, among His disciples, it had to be different. That's why He said, "I have set the example, and you should do for each other exactly what I have done for you" (John 13:15, CEV).

The Bible includes many stories of God's people being instruments of service. Through service, Joseph saved countless lives in Egypt and the surrounding region. Elijah helped the widow of Zarephath and her son, eventually saving them from starvation (1 Kings 17:8–16). Tabitha, also known as Dorcas of Joppa, "was full of good works and charitable deeds" (Acts 9:36).

Perhaps one of the best examples of service was Martha, who was Mary and Lazarus's sister. Jesus and His disciples visited their home often for rest and loving care. The two sisters showed a willingness to serve because of their sincere love for God's truth. They were warm hearted, tender, and made their home a haven of rest for the weary Lord and His companions. This shows that the mission field of service can be as close as the home in which you live. Harmony would grow in every home if Jesus' lesson of servant leadership were put into practice.

Oneness

Another dynamic of the marital relationship is the mystery of oneness. God declares that two should become one, but which one? True oneness in marriage cannot occur by having one person's identity subjugated by the other—one person's identity can never be lost in that of the other. And yet a lasting relationship involves compromise, which is an accommodation of autonomy. Certain compromises are made for the benefit of both—for the good of "us."

God intends that we come together with our wonderful diversity and form a powerful oneness in marriage. Four times we find these words in the Bible: "A man shall leave his father and mother and be joined to his wife, and they shall become one flesh" (Genesis 2:24; see also Matthew 19:5; Mark 10:8; Ephesians 5:31). It is as if God does not want us to miss the point.

In 1 Corinthians 12 and 14, Paul describes the body of Christ as being one (oneness) but made up of many individual parts; each is unique in its own function. It is one body with wonderful diversity. A marriage is a team of allies, working toward a common goal. Their unity does not generate uniformity; it powerfully creates oneness in the midst of diversity.

Unity in ministry

Jesus' work of developing disciples is not finished yet. Paul writes, "God planned for us to do good things and to live as he has always wanted us to live. That's why he sent Christ to make us what we are" (Ephesians 2:10, CEV). These "good things" are service to others. Whenever we serve others in any way, we are actually serving God and fulfilling one of His purposes (Matthew 25:34–45; Ephesians 6:7; Colossians 3:23, 24).

God has been preparing us for leadership in His cause before we were born, and all He asks of us now is to respond by giving ourselves back to Him and to His service (Jeremiah 1:5; Romans 12:1, 2). We do not know when we may be called into action. It could be at work, at church, around the community, for a planned event, or when we least expect it. All we know is that God can use us when He presents us with the opportunity to serve others.

Communicating and modeling the value of service should be

a high priority for parents. Perhaps one of the greatest concerns parents have is how to make sure their children remain connected to God and His church. We pray for them, teach them memory verses, take them to church, but what else can we do to help them learn to serve Jesus and others? We noted the following in the foreword to *Discipleship and Service: Reaching Families for Jesus*, the 2018 Planbook for the Department of Family Ministries:

> [Mark] DeVries writes of the dramatic importance of parents in the faith formation of their children, explaining that when parents talk about faith and involve them in service activities it doubles and sometimes triples their children's chances of living out their faith as adults [Mark DeVries, *Family-Based Youth Ministry*, rev. and expanded ed. (Downers Grove, IL: InterVarsity Press, 2004), 63]. [Ben] Freudenburg cites studies conducted by his denomination that show four family practices that are particularly important in helping young people grow in faith (both in childhood and adolescence): (1) talking about faith with their mother; (2) talking about faith with their father; (3) having family devotions or prayer; and (4) doing family projects to help other people. Unfortunately, fewer than one-third of the youth reported any of these activities as happening often in the past or currently in their homes [Ben Freudenburg and Rick Lawrence, *The Family Friendly Church* (Loveland, CO: Group Pub., 1998), 17]. The Valuegenesis[4] studies conducted among Adventist young people also confirm the important role parents play in transmitting their faith to their children not only by talking about [service] but by joining them in helping-projects in their community or missionary endeavors [V. Bailey Gillespie, Michael J. Donahue, Barry Gane, and Ed Boyatt, *Valuegenesis Ten Years Later: A Study of Two Generations* (Riverside, CA: Hancock Center Pub, 2004), 255–273].[5]

Seasons of Unity

Unity in ministry and unity in mission keep children actively engaged in the life of the church. As individuals, they will not think identically as their parents, but joining their parents in service will teach them to help and bless others.

Family unity

If the goal of family life is unity, how can we achieve it? Here are some suggestions:[6]

1. Communicate. It is vital that family members spend time in communication about their plans, problems, issues they are facing, and goals for the future. Allow each family member to openly express their views and their feelings.

2. Listen to each other. One of the most neglected elements of healthy communication is the ability to listen attentively. As your spouse or children speak, try to consider his or her perspective. Active listening lets the other person know, especially your children, that they are important and that their opinions and feelings matter.

3. Share household responsibilities. Have a conversation with your spouse to decide what responsibilities each member of the family should have, and then communicate those expectations to your children. If you present a unified front when you propose this idea to your children, you are more likely to get a positive reaction.

4. Assign specific chores, considering each child's age and abilities.

5. Establish routines. Routine and consistency help children to feel safe and secure.

6. Seek spiritual experiences. When parents choose not to attend church or send their children instead of going together, they are sending the very strong message that church and spirituality are not that important. Attending church as a family reinforces what you are trying to teach them about God. In addition, read the Bible and other spiritual literature that supports your family's belief system and inspires them to be better. When you reinforce a shared value system, you create a spiritual culture within the family and teach your children that they are part of a greater whole—God's family around the world.

7. Have fun together. This should go without saying, yet many families do not make time to just have fun. At least once a month, go on a family outing. These do not have to be expensive or complicated. Perhaps you can go for a walk, visit a local zoo, or go to a museum. Taking regular family vacations is good for your health and is a wonderful way to create positive family memories. Every family can work together to develop lasting happiness. "It is truly wonderful when relatives live together in peace" (Psalm 133:1, CEV).

For further consideration

1. What are specific examples of servant leadership from the life and ministry of Jesus? In what ways can we imitate Him? In what ways can we adapt His methods to suit our personality, talents, or training?

2. Read Matthew 25:31–40. Are the activities listed by Jesus the only ways in which we can be of service to others? In what other ways can you be a servant to the least of Christ's brethren?

3. Make a list of ten actions you can take to be a better servant to your parents, your spouse, or your children. Prioritize those actions, and practice a new one each week.

4. Does having unity mean we cannot have different opinions? In what areas must we be united?

---

1. Leo Tolstoy, *Anna Karenina*, vol. 1, trans. Nathan Haskell Dole (New York: Thomas Y. Crowell, 1899), 1.

2. Ellen G. White, *The Adventist Home* (Washington, DC: Review and Herald®, 1952), 179

3. Ellen G. White, *Selected Messages*, vol.1 (Washington, DC: Review and Herald®, 1958), 259.

4. " 'Valuegenesis' is a research study into the faith and values of young people attending Seventh-day Adventist high schools in North America in the three areas of family, school, and church. The first survey was conducted in 1990, a second major survey was conducted in 2000, and a third is taking place in 2010. Related studies

also termed 'Valuegenesis' have been conducted in other countries." Wikipedia, s.v. "Valuegenesis," last modified July 21, 2018, https://en.wikipedia.org/wiki/Valuegenesis, quoted in Claudio Consuegra and Pamela Consuegra, foreword to *Discipleship and Service: Reaching Families for Jesus*, North American Division ed., ed. Claudio Consuegra and Pamela Consuegra (Silver Spring, MD: General Conference of Seventh-day Adventists, 2017), i, ii, http://www.nadfamily.org/site/1/docs/FM_Planbook_2018_-_Interior_Pages_Color.pdf.

5. Claudio Consuegra and Pamela Consuegra, foreword to *Discipleship and Service: Reaching Families for Jesus*, North American Division ed., ed. Claudio Consuegra and Pamela Consuegra (Silver Spring, MD: General Conference of Seventh-day Adventists, 2017), i, ii, http://www.nadfamily.org/site/1/docs/FM_Planbook_2018_-_Interior_Pages_Color.pdf.

6. Adapted from Lynn Scoresby, "7 Effective Ways to Build Family Unity," Famifi, January 7, 2013, https://www.famifi.com/995/7-effective-ways-to-build-family-unity.

CHAPTER 8

Seasons of Parenting

Most mothers can identify with Hannah, Samuel's mother, and Mary, the mother of Jesus. They understand the maternal heart. During the nine months of pregnancy, a close bond develops between a mother and her child. While fathers do not have the intimate prenatal contact with their children, they are still filled with awe and pride when they hold their newborn children, who are "flesh of our flesh and bones of our bones" (see Genesis 2:23). Of course, countless couples yearn to have their own child but remain childless for various reasons. Still others, blessed with parents' hearts, choose to adopt.

Early in our marriage, after our first daughter was born, we lost two babies to miscarriages. While we rationalized that perhaps it was for the best and wondered if something had been wrong with those two babies, the pain of losing two precious unborn lives was at times almost unbearable, especially for their mother.

As each little one grew inside her, so did her hopes. Day by day she imagined what these children would be like. She could hardly wait to feel her babies kick. Life was good and full of joy and expectation.

But one day everything changed, as the precious life ended. A little over a year later, the nightmare happened for the second time. The joy that had sprouted after learning she was pregnant now dissolved into newfound grief. So many questions bombarded our minds. Was God playing with our feelings? Why would He give us a precious gift only to snatch it away? Her arms ached for the baby she would never hold, wondering if she would ever recover.

We are grateful that in our case she became pregnant again and gave birth nine months later to a beautiful, healthy baby girl who is now a general surgeon. We look forward to the day when we will be reunited and see our unborn babies grow into the fullness of health and life forever.

Childless parenting

Women tend to be nurturing from the time they are little girls. They play with dolls, holding them close to their chests, talking to them as if they were children. While much of this behavior may mimic their own mothers, God wired females with this nurturing, caring, loving attitude. He compares His love to that of a mother for her children:

> "Could a mother forget a child
>   who nurses at her breast?
> Could she fail to love an infant
>   who came from her own body?
> Even if a mother could forget,
>   I will never forget you" (Isaiah 49:15, CEV).

It is just as inconceivable that a mother would forget her child as it is that God would forget His children.

Imagine, then, what it must be like for a tenderhearted, nurturing woman who longs for children not to have a child to love and care for. Rachel, Jacob's wife, experienced this pain when she saw her sister enjoying motherhood. Her own arms and heart were empty, and her agony led her to make a demand of

Seasons of Parenting

Jacob, "Give me children, or else I die!" (Genesis 30:1). She even followed the custom of the time and presented Jacob with her servant Bilhah, so her maidservant could conceive and give Rachel a baby she could call her own. Considering her emptiness and pain, we can also understand her great joy at the birth of her firstborn, Joseph, and later his brother Benjamin.

Hannah, Samuel's mother, also went through a dark period of barrenness. She cried every year her husband, Elkanah, would go to the temple for the sacrifices. Unfortunately, she could not present a sacrifice on behalf of her children. "Hannah was brokenhearted and was crying as she prayed" (1 Samuel 1:10, CEV). Eli the priest saw her and, thinking she was drunk, chastised her. Looking back, we know her story turned out well with the birth of Samuel. But how many have never had a child of their own? Praise God for the many parents who have not had their own biological children but who have opened their hearts and homes to children they have chosen. Their love is not and cannot be limited to their own natural children.

Single parenting

The Bible does not directly address single parenting, but there are many examples of God's love and gentle interaction with fathers, mothers, widows, and their children. God knows each parent fully and understands the situation completely.

Difficult circumstances often place people in the position of raising children alone. Many of them are innocent victims of a world wracked by war and terrorism. Spouses may die as a result of disease, an accident, or even by their own hands, leaving the other parent to raise the children by themselves.

The good news is that the Bible contains words of encouragement for single parents. Here are a few such verses:[1]

- When you are overwhelmed: "But those who trust in the LORD for help will find their strength renewed. . . . They will run and not get weary; they will walk and not grow

weak" (Isaiah 40:31, GNT).
- When you are tired: "Come to me, all of you who are tired from carrying heavy loads, and I will give you rest" (Matthew 11:28, GNT).
- When you feel alone: "I will be with you always, even until the end of the world" (Matthew 28:20, CEV).
- When you are worried about money: "And with all his abundant wealth through Christ Jesus, my God will supply all your needs" (Philippians 4:19, GNT).
- When you need wisdom: "Trust in the LORD with all your heart. Never rely on what you think you know. Remember the LORD in everything you do, and he will show you the right way" (Proverbs 3:5, 6, GNT).

The joy and responsibility of parenting

Experts today recognize four styles of parenting: authoritarian, authoritative, permissive, and uninvolved. Here's a brief description of each.[2]

1. Authoritarian parenting. This type of parent believes his or her children "should follow the rules without exception" and do not "allow kids to get involved in problem-solving challenges or obstacles. Instead, they make the rules and enforce the consequences with little regard for a child's opinion." Authoritarian parents "are not interested in negotiating and their focus is on obedience." As a result, they "may use punishments instead of discipline. So rather than teach a child how to make better choices," they are often focused on making a child suffer for his mistakes.

"Children who grow up with strict authoritarian parents tend to follow rules much of the time," but they may develop self-esteem problems and, eventually, "become hostile or aggressive." Studies show they may also become good liars, as they become conditioned to lie to avoid punishment.[3]

2. Authoritative parenting. These parents work to ensure they have a positive relationship with their child, explaining the reasoning behind their rules. They enforce rules and give consequences but take their child's feelings into consideration. Authoritative parents often use logical consequences that teach life lessons and "use positive discipline strategies" to prevent behavior problems and "reinforce good behavior."

Children raised with authoritative or democratic discipline "tend to be happy and successful." Because they have been included in the decision-making process, they are "more likely to be good at making decisions and evaluating safety risks on their own." Researchers have found kids who have authoritative parents are most likely to become responsible adults who feel comfortable expressing their opinions.[4]

3. Permissive parenting. Permissive parents tend to "set rules but rarely enforce them" or impose consequences for breaking them. These parents believe their child will learn best if they do not interfere in what they do.

Permissive parents are lenient and "often only step in when there's a serious problem." Even when they attempt to deliver consequences, which is not very often, they give in if their child begs or "promises to be good." These types of parents want to be their child's friend but, in the process, forget that they are their child's parent.

Children who "grow up with permissive parents are more likely to struggle academically" because their parents "usually don't put much effort into discouraging poor choices or bad behavior." These children "may exhibit more behavioral problems," since they have not been taught to "appreciate authority and rules." These children often suffer from low self-esteem and may report a lingering sadness. This mind-set puts them "at higher risk for health problems, like obesity, because permissive parents struggle to limit junk food intake" and do not always teach hygiene habits, such as brushing one's teeth, bathing, and wearing clean clothes.[5]

4. Uninvolved parenting. Uninvolved parents can be considered neglectful. They do not ask their child about school or homework, seldom know where their child is or who he or she is with, and in general terms, do not spend much time with their child. "Uninvolved parents expect children to raise themselves. They don't devote much time or energy to meeting children's basic needs."

How could a parent be so uncaring? "A parent with mental health issues or substance abuse problems, for example, may not be able to care for a child's physical or emotional needs on a consistent basis." Some "uninvolved parents lack knowledge about child development." Others are "overwhelmed with other problems, like work, paying bills, and managing a household."

Because children of uninvolved parents receive little guidance, nurture, or parental attention, they often "struggle with self-esteem issues." This leads to behavioral problems and poor performance in school.[6]

If you are a parent, this advice is worth careful consideration. Are you giving your children enough love and attention so that they will grow up emotionally healthy? Are you involved in their lives? Do you listen carefully to what they tell you? Are you showing them by example how to relate to their heavenly Father?

Parenting as disciple making

The New Testament command to make disciples comes from the Great Commission. As Jesus was about to return to heaven, He told His disciples, "Go therefore and make disciples of all the nations, baptizing them in the name of the Father and of the Son and of the Holy Spirit, teaching them to observe all things that I have commanded you; and lo, I am with you always, even to the end of the age" (Matthew 28:19, 20). Since then, the church has been God's agency in the world, making disciples of Jesus. But as parents, we have not always remembered that our children are our first responsibility and that our primary goal should be leading them to be disciples of Jesus. As Ellen White clearly states, "Our work for Christ is to begin with the family, in the home.... There is no missionary field more important than this."[7]

Seasons of Parenting

Parents need to shift their focus of ministry to the work of disciple making in their own homes. Once they have done that, the family can become an evangelistic agency for others. "Our time, our strength, and our energies belong to God; and if they are consecrated to his service, our light will shine. It will affect first and most strongly those in our own homes, who are most intimately associated with us; but it will extend beyond the home, even to 'the world.' "[8]

Fighting for your prodigal child

After some two thousand years of reading the parable of the prodigal son, it has become so familiar that it may have lost its sharp edge. We cheer the return of the prodigal and hail the love of his father; but when Jesus told this story, it was probably not received with much applause. Keep in mind that the prodigal's request for his portion of the inheritance while his father still lived was the equivalent of saying, "I wish you were dead, Dad! I wish you were dead, so I could get what I have coming to me." It was shocking then, and it is shocking now. To make matters worse, the ungrateful son squanders the money in a frenzy of what Jesus discreetly called loose living.

Dennis Rainey reminds us that "the core meaning of the word prodigal is 'waste.' The famous prodigal son from Jesus' parable in Luke 15:11–32 not only wasted the material possessions of his inheritance and much of his life, but he also did much worse. He wasted, through rebellion and foolishness, his precious relationship with his father."[9] "The father's heart was broken as was the relationship between him and his son. So much more than an inheritance was lost."[10]

Among the many lessons in the story of the prodigal son, here are a few that stand out:

1. *Letting go.* The father in the story knew it was time to let go. His son had made his decision, and even though it broke the father's heart, the decision was his son's to make.

As concerning as it is, the time is coming when your son or daughter will make their own decisions. Yes, you will always be there to offer guidance, encouragement, and support. But ultimately, they will soon be out on their own, making their own decisions.

2. *We are that prodigal son or daughter.* It may be easy to see your child as a prodigal, but have you ever considered the fact that you are also a prodigal? Acknowledge your own status as a "prodigal son." It is easy to become so wrapped up in this story that we forget each of us has also been a prodigal son or daughter. We have made mistakes and have saddened our Father God. But He has never stopped loving us. Rather, He anticipated our homecoming and made preparations so that, like the father in the parable, He could welcome us home with all the best.

3. *Forgive.* Extend forgiveness to your child in the same way that God has forgiven you!

4. *Never stop praying.* Never give up, and never stop praying for your child. Your goal for your child is eternity and God is able![11]

For further consideration

1. Where should children be in your priority list? In relationship to them, what place should those outside the family have?

2. What does Ellen G. White mean when she writes, "Teach them [your children] to yield their will to yours"?[12] What is the difference between being in control and being controlling?

---

1. Adapted from Sarah Ortiz, "6 Bible Verses for Single Parents," *Blog.Bible*, September 19, 2015, http://blog.bible/bible-blog/entry/6-bible-verses-for-single-parents.

2. Adapted from Amy Morin, "4 Types of Parenting Styles and Their Effects on Kids," Verywell Family, last updated March 29, 2018, https://www.verywell.com/types-of-parenting-styles-1095045.

3. Morin, "4 Types of Parenting."

4. Morin, "4 Types of Parenting."

5. Morin, "4 Types of Parenting."

6. Morin, "4 Types of Parenting."

7. Ellen G. White, *The Adventist Home* (Washington, DC: Review and Herald®, 1952), 35.

8. Ellen G. White, "Christian Homes," *Signs of the Times*, January 14, 1886, 1.

9. Dennis Rainey, "Loving the Prodigal Child," Family Life, accessed August 20, 2018, http://www.familylife.com/articles/topics/parenting/challenges/anger-and-rebellion/loving-the-prodigal-child.

10. Claudio Consuegra and Pamela Consuegra, *Help! I'm a Parent* (Lincoln, NE: AdventSource, 2017).

11. Consuegra and Consuegra, *Help! I'm a Parent*.

12. Ellen G. White, *Child Guidance* (Washington, DC: Review and Herald®, 1954), 230.

CHAPTER 9

Seasons of Loss

Adam and Eve experienced loss from the moment they disobeyed God. In the wake of their mistaken choices, seasons of loss began for all their descendants. Billions have died, and countless others have suffered losses—marriage, jobs, health, freedom, and sadly, all hope and faith in God. Such heartache would be overwhelming if not for the heartening promise that "weeping may endure for a night, but joy comes in the morning" (Psalm 30:5).

Loss of health

The Bible has plenty to say about sickness and death. Satan "caused painful sores to break out all over Job's body—from head to toe" (Job 2:7, CEV); Naaman had leprosy; Hezekiah was near death (2 Kings 20:1); an unnamed woman suffered from bleeding for twelve long years (Matthew 9:20); and the list goes on. We ache because we live in a fallen world. When sin entered, so did death, but it also brought chronic pain, illness, and disease, which are all a form of death. When faced with a chronic or terminal illness, we may experience shock, anger, and/or despair and may even feel like shouting,

> My God, my God, why have you deserted me?

Family Seasons

> Why are you so far away?
> Won't you listen to my groans
>   and come to my rescue? (Psalm 22:1, CEV).

Just as David did, we would do well to take our questions, our anger, and our pain to God.

As much as we may groan in our suffering, it often strengthens us. God told Isaiah, "I have refined you, but not as silver; I have tested you in the furnace of affliction" (Isaiah 48:10). James adds that trials produce patience, growth, and maturity (James 1:2–4). And ultimately, "all things work together for good" as suffering conforms us to God's image (Romans 8:28; see also verse 29). Sometimes we want these verses to say that God will bring good out of everything, because He can and does remove pain from our lives. But these verses do not suggest He will remove all of our health challenges. Rather, if we allow Him, He will use our trials to prepare us for eternity with Him.

The apostle Paul suffered from an ailment that some have suggested may have been poor eyesight. Eugene Peterson's Bible paraphrase renders Paul's struggle this way:

> If I had a mind to brag a little, I could probably do it without looking ridiculous, and I'd still be speaking plain truth all the way. But I'll spare you. I don't want anyone imagining me as anything other than the fool you'd encounter if you saw me on the street or heard me talk.
>
> Because of the extravagance of those revelations, and so I wouldn't get a big head, I was given the gift of a handicap to keep me in constant touch with my limitations. Satan's angel did his best to get me down; what he in fact did was push me to my knees. No danger then of walking around high and mighty! At first I didn't think of it as a gift, and begged God to remove it. Three times I did that, and then he told me,
>
> My grace is enough; it's all you need.

> My strength comes into its own in your weakness.
> Once I heard that, I was glad to let it happen. I quit focusing on the handicap and began appreciating the gift. It was a case of Christ's strength moving in on my weakness (2 Corinthians 12:6–9, *The Message*).

It may be difficult to believe that God's grace is all we need when languishing in the midst of pain and suffering. Nevertheless, we may find hope in the knowledge that sickness and death will not last forever.

Loss of trust

Healthy relationships are built on trust. When that trust is violated, the very foundations of the relationship are shaken. The journey toward healing after trust is broken can only continue when there is genuine sorrow on the part of the betrayer. Without true repentance, it is like building a brick wall without cement. Without genuine sorrow and forgiveness, marital reconciliation is superficial and unsatisfying for both spouses.

"It's natural to be hurt by cheating and dishonesty, but it's not okay to use the past against your partner. Trust is something we decide to give, rather than being something that can be earned back. . . . If you're unsure whether or not you can trust your partner, think about what it would take for you to trust them again." If you think you will regain trust in your spouse by being jealous, by "checking up on them or trying to control their actions, then you aren't really trusting them." Instead, begin by forgiving them, that is, releasing them to God's judgment and thus freeing yourself from the feelings of anger that keep you a prisoner to the hurt of the past. If you are not married and "you feel you cannot trust your partner again, then it might be time to consider whether or not the relationship is right for you."[1]

Intimate partner violence (IPV) damages and may even destroy the trust upon which a healthy relationship is built. After all, how can a person trust a spouse who has emotionally hurt, verbally attacked, or physically injured him or her? Trusting a physically abusive person may not only be unwise but unsafe for the spouse and his or her children. In cases where IPV takes place, the victim may forgive the batterer, but the relationship may be damaged beyond repair.

Loss of freedom

Visiting a jail or prison can be unsettling. Hearing the heavy doors slam shut behind you or standing behind the iron bars is intimidating. But many are held captive without ever seeing the inside of a prison cell.

If asked to name some addictions, what would you say? Perhaps you might list such things as drugs, alcohol, tobacco, gambling, pornography, sex, and food (Galatians 5:19–21). The genesis of addiction is complicated and involves many psychological, emotional, and biochemical factors. Gradually, it begins to dictate your behavior and you are unable to stop even when you know it is harming you. While enjoying your freedom to choose, you become a slave to your addiction—you actually lose your freedom. Peter offers a simple explanation of addiction and its results: "They promise freedom to everyone. But they are merely slaves of filthy living, because people are slaves of whatever controls them" (2 Peter 2:19, CEV). By becoming a slave to that which controls you, you have in essence lost your freedom.

The apostle James describes how addictions develop: "We are tempted by our own desires that drag us off and trap us. Our desires make us sin, and when sin is finished with us, it leaves us dead" (James 1:14, 15, CEV). What may seem like a harmless experiment leads one gradual step at a time to full-blown entrapment. The apostle Paul explains, "Don't you know that you are slaves of anyone you obey? You can be slaves of sin and die, or you can be obedient slaves of God and be acceptable to him" (Romans 6:16, CEV).

Addictions and sin begin in our minds and take root in our hearts. The way to eradicate sin from our lives is more than an exercise in behavior modification. The only lasting solution to the problem of sin and addiction is receiving a new heart: "Because we belong to Christ Jesus, we have killed our selfish feelings and desires" (Galatians 5:24, CEV). Paul also explains what it means to die to that sinful, addictive nature so that we can live for Christ (Romans 6:8–13); he then adds, "Let the Lord Jesus Christ be as near to you as the clothes you wear. Then you won't try to satisfy your selfish desires" (Romans 13:14, CEV).

Many have suffered as a result of their addictions. They have become slaves to their desires and have lost their money, their jobs, their health, their families, and their freedom. But Jesus came to give us freedom from sin and all our addictions: "If the Son makes you free, you shall be free indeed" (John 8:36). Jesus also promised He would always be with us, so we do not have to wage this war alone (Matthew 28:20; Isaiah 43:2). In fact, we must remember that the battle is the Lord's, and He promises total victory (1 Samuel 17:47; 1 Peter 1:3–9). Today you can travel the road to victory over any addiction and receive the freedom God wants for you.

Even if we are not imprisoned by an addiction, we are never really safe without God's help. In Eugene Peterson's paraphrase of 1 Corinthians 10:12, Paul says, "Don't be so naive and self-confident. You're not exempt. You could fall flat on your face as easily as anyone else. Forget about self-confidence; it's useless. Cultivate God-confidence" (*The Message*). Ellen White also has a warning that is pertinent to all of us: "No man is safe for a day or an hour without prayer. . . . While we must constantly guard against the devices of Satan, we should pray in faith continually: 'Lead us not into temptation.' "[2]

Loss of life

> Grief is a multifaceted response to loss, particularly to the loss of someone or something that has died. . . . Although conventionally focused on the emotional response to loss,

it also has physical, cognitive, behavioral, social, cultural, spiritual and philosophical dimensions. . . .

Grief is a natural response to loss. It is the emotional suffering one feels when something or someone the individual loves is taken away.[3]

Some losses are physical and tangible, such as the death of one of our children, our parents, or our spouse. Other losses are more abstract, like the social interaction we miss when our spouse dies.

For years, we have known that terminally ill people usually go through five stages in the process of dying—denial, anger, bargaining, depression, and acceptance. Denial, the first of these stages, usually occurs when people are told they have a terminal illness. When we hear the news, "we are in a state of shock and denial. We go numb. We wonder how we can go on, if we can go on, why we should go on. We try to find a way to simply get through each day." During the second stage, people are angry—with themselves, with the doctors, and even with God. While some try to suppress or deny their anger, it is a necessary step in their journey toward acceptance and peace. In the third stage, "before a loss, it seems like you will do anything if only your loved one would be spared. 'Please God,' you bargain, 'I will never be angry at my wife again if you'll just let her live.'" "After bargaining, our attention moves squarely into the present. Empty feelings present themselves, and grief enters our lives on a deeper level, deeper than we ever imagined. This depressive stage feels as though it will last forever." Finally, some people arrive at the final stage—acceptance. It does not mean they like this new reality or that it is OK, but eventually they accept it. They learn to live with it.[4]

Terminally ill people are not the only ones that experience these stages; their loved ones do too. When the person dies, we also feel the emotions that accompany each stage. In the end, "it is the new norm with which we must learn to live. We must try to live now in a world where our loved one is missing. In resisting this new norm, at first many people want to maintain life as it was before a loved one died. In time, through bits and pieces of acceptance, however, we see that we cannot maintain the past intact." Eventually, we get to the point where we reorganize our lives so loss is an important part of it, rather than its center.[5] There is no right or a wrong way to grieve; everyone grieves differently. But as Christians, we can find a rich source of comfort and strength in God's Word (Psalm 34:17–20; Isaiah 40:1–31; Matthew 5:4; 2 Corinthians 1:3–5).

"People often think of the stages as lasting weeks or months. They forget that the stages are responses to feelings that can last for minutes or hours as we flip in and out of one and then another. We do not enter and leave each individual stage in a linear fashion. We may feel one, then another and back again to the first one."[6] Many of these stages overlap, occur together, or may be missed altogether.

Loss of hope

What do you do when you find yourself at the end of your rope and there seems to be no way out? Hagar found herself in that situation. Once before she had tried to run away from her abusive situation (Genesis 16:6–16). Now she was summarily dismissed with some bread and a skin of water to survive in the wilderness (Genesis 21:14). Hopeless, with death staring her and her son in the eye, God heard her plea and rescued them from certain death (verses 15–21).

When you are in the dark pit of despair, thoughts may come to mind to harm yourself or to end it all.

> Perhaps you are convinced that life is not worth living. You feel like your world is collapsing in on you. . . .
>
> . . . You can't see any solution to your problems. You're not looking forward to anything. The future seems empty.
>
> God's perspective on your life is different. Your life is precious to Him. He knows everything about you—even how many hairs are on your head.[7]

He promises,

> "Fear not, for I am with you;
> Be not dismayed, for I am your God.
> I will strengthen you,
> Yes, I will help you,
> I will uphold you with My righteous right hand" (Isaiah 41:10).

If we hold on to the hope that our Lord offers and neither give up nor give in, His light will shine in the darkness of our lives. David writes, "Weeping may endure for a night, but joy comes in the morning" (Psalm 30:5). When everything seems hopeless, wait patiently on God. He knows all and will bring joy out of suffering.

For further consideration

1. What is the benefit of contemplating and recounting the mercies of God while you are passing through sorrow and affliction?

2. Keep a gratitude journal. When you think about one of God's mercies, blessings, or answers to prayer, write it down immediately. During difficult times and dark spiritual valleys, remind yourself of God's generosity, love, and kindness.

---

1. "Trust," National Domestic Violence Hotline, accessed August 20, 2018, https://www.thehotline.org/healthy-relationships/trust/.
2. Ellen G. White, *Darkness Before Dawn* (Nampa, ID: Pacific Press®, 1997), 12.
3. Wikipedia, s.v. "Grief," last modified August 15, 2018, https://en.wikipedia.org/wiki/Grief.
4. David Kessler, "The Five Stages of Grief," accessed August 20, 2018, Grief.com, https://grief.com/the-five-stages-of-grief/.
5. Kessler, "The Five Stages of Grief."
6. Kessler, "The Five Stages of Grief."
7. David Powlison, *I Just Want to Die: Replacing Suicidal Thoughts With Hope* (Greensboro, NC: New Growth Press, 2010), 3.

CHAPTER 10

Seasons of Conflict

Families matter to God, and He longs for them to be happy and harmonious. Unfortunately, the moment Adam and Eve ate of the forbidden fruit, sin and conflict entered their home (Genesis 3:1–19). The jealousy and hatred of their firstborn led him to kill his brother—the first murder in human history (Genesis 4).

> Adam's life was one of sorrow, humility, and contrition. When he left Eden, the thought that he must die filled him with horror. He was first made acquainted with the reality of death in the human family when Cain, his firstborn son, became the murderer of his brother. Filled with the keenest remorse for his own sin, and doubly bereaved in the death of Abel and the rejection of Cain, Adam was bowed down with anguish. He witnessed the widespreading corruption that was finally to cause the destruction of the world by a flood; and though the sentence of death pronounced upon him by His Maker had at first appeared terrible, yet after beholding for nearly a thousand years the results of sin, he felt that it was merciful in God to bring to an end a life of suffering and sorrow.[1]

Family Seasons

Even in the best and godliest of families, conflict is inevitable. Controlling in-laws, wayward teens, sibling rivalry, or jealous stepchildren can turn a happy home into a war zone. Simple things such as trash duty, homework, and chores become easy flash points. But relatively minor issues can generally be resolved with minimal interruption to family life. Other issues, however, can be a lot more challenging and disruptive to family life. The mother-in-law whose abuse and manipulation threatens to destroy a marriage; the mentally ill father who abuses his children; the son who abandons his religious upbringing for a promiscuous lifestyle; or the daughter who becomes a substance abuser—all these situations are real and, sadly, can occur even in Christian families. Resolution may be quick and straightforward, but the problem may linger for months or even years.

Conflict

Benjamin Franklin was on target when he stated, "An ounce of prevention is worth a pound of cure." "Family conflicts can seem like the most intense disagreements because they involve the people to whom you are closest. Family of origin relationships carry a long history"[2] and issues can easily span generations. When two people marry, these two histories often compete or collide, which can bring about disagreements families must deal with.

> In-laws sometimes bring a whole new bag of potential conflicts because of cultural and political differences. At the same time, your immediate family is made up of the people who demand daily attention. While you may not always agree with family members, you can avoid conflict by setting boundaries and choosing your battles wisely.
>
> Step 1[:] Set boundaries for conflict resolution. . . . Disagreements and debate are healthy components of most relationships and need not be completely avoided as long as everyone present sticks to preset rules. For example, when voices begin to rise, you may elect to end the

discussion and agree to continue it when tempers subside.

Step 2[:] Choose your battles. . . . It's better to let certain issues slide rather than make a big deal about every difference, especially around the holidays when tension is high and family togetherness is expected.

Step 3[:] Encourage your family to end an ongoing conflict by setting up a meeting for that purpose. . . . A family can learn to collaborate to end conflicts. Appoint one person to moderate the discussion and keep talking until you come up with a solution to the conflict.

Step 4[:] Remain neutral when a touchy subject comes up. . . . The family member who can stay neutral during family conflicts can help each family member articulate [his or] her thoughts. You then can rephrase the sentiments to try to come to mutual understandings and find compromise. . . .

The past is full of land mines that most often are best left buried. Avoid stepping on those mines by refusing to bring up past incidents and wrongs. Reliving the past can create conflict even when none exist in the moment. Children are sponges and will be watching as you interact with your family members. Remember that you are teaching them how to handle disagreements and anger when you become involved in family conflicts.[3]

Dealing with destructive conflict

In Matthew 18:15–17, we find Jesus' outline of dealing with conflict. Often we avoid taking these steps and instead tell someone else how others have offended or hurt us. If a third person allows himself or herself to be brought into this situation, a triangle forms (in psychology, it is referred to as *triangulation*). Siblings bring a parent into their conflict, members of the church rope the pastor into their squabbles, and coworkers speak to their supervisor, rather than to each other, about their disagreements.

While, in general terms, conflict is very much a part of life, some of it stems from differences in personality, opinions, likes, dreams, and aspirations. But there is also a type of conflict caused by deep-seated selfishness, anger, hatred, or total disregard for the other person. This source of conflict can be destructive.

> Satan is constantly seeking to introduce distrust, alienation, and malice among God's people. We shall often be tempted to feel that our rights are invaded, even when there is no real cause for such feelings. Those whose love for self is stronger than their love for Christ and His cause will place their own interests first and will resort to almost any expedient to guard and maintain them. Even many who appear to be conscientious Christians are hindered by pride and self-esteem from going privately to those whom they think in error, that they may talk with them in the spirit of Christ and pray together for one another. When they think themselves injured by their brethren, some will even go to law instead of following the Saviour's rule.[4]

From Jesus' words in Matthew 18:15–17, we glean three general principles that can be applied when dealing with destructive conflict. First of all, "speak up. 'If your brother sins against you, go and show him his fault, just between the two of you' (Matt. 18:15 NIV). . . . Pursuing peace might mean risking conflict in order to bring about a genuine peace (Ps. 34:14; Heb. 12:14 NIV). Speaking up is very different from venting, which can have negative consequences. We should speak the truth to someone in love after we have spent time praying and preparing for our time together. Approach that person in gentleness and with humility (Gal. 6:1 NIV)."[5] It is also important to approach someone privately instead of confronting him or her in public or telling others about the situation before speaking with the person.

The second principle we can deduce from Jesus' instructions is to "stand up. 'But if he will not listen, take one or two others along, so that "every matter may be established by the testimony of two or three witnesses" ' (Matt. 18:16 NIV). . . . When others are blind to their sin, God calls us to enlist the help of others."[6]

If the first two attempts fail to resolve the issue, then the third step tells us to stand back. " 'If he refuses to listen even to the church, treat him as you would a pagan or a tax collector (Matt. 18:17 NIV),' says Jesus. . . . When we step back from the relationship, it helps minimize the damage and gives the other person time to reflect on his behavior and the relationship."[7]

When we skip these steps, we are as guilty as the ones with whom we have conflict. While every issue may not be resolved in a satisfactory way, we are nevertheless called to act lovingly and patiently toward others, even if the conflict cannot be resolved (1 Corinthians 4:12; Romans 13:10).

The role of anger in conflict

Though difficult to control, anger is an important and legitimate emotion. In fact, even Jesus displayed strong displeasure at how the people of His time were treating God's temple (Matthew 21:12).

In dealing with anger, it helps to put things in perspective.

> When we are battling anger, we must realize that "we wrestle not against flesh and blood, but against principalities, against powers, against the rulers of the darkness of this world, against spiritual wickedness in high places" (Ephesians 6:12 [KJV]). When Satan makes you angry, remember that he's trying to keep you from receiving the will of God in your life.
>
> In 2 Timothy 4:5, Paul told Timothy to be calm, cool and collected and to keep performing the duties of his ministry. That's good advice for all of us. When we get angry, we should calm down and start doing what God has called us to do.
>
> You can be bitter or better, it's up to you! If you're mad

about something, instead of letting it ruin you, turn it into something good. Overcome evil and anger by praying for those who hurt and abuse you. Forgive them and be a blessing to them. It may not be easy at first, but when you make the decision and stick with it, God will take care of the rest.[8]

It is no secret that there is a direct relationship between anger and conflict. We have the choice to allow anger, which is a normal emotion, to control us to the point of hurting someone else; or we can choose to "be angry, and do not sin" (Ephesians 4:26). Paul's counsel is "do not let the sun go down on your wrath" (verse 27), which has been understood to mean that all conflict must be resolved before going to bed. A parallel passage may help us to understand better Paul's intent. King David wrote, "Be angry, and do not sin. Meditate within your heart on your bed, and be still" (Psalm 4:4). It may be better to keep from saying anything that is hurtful, give yourself time to pray, calm down, carefully assess the situation, and try to resolve the issue in the light of a new day.

Conflict, abuse, power, and control

The Bible states that "an abusive person does not know love and does not know God." (See 1 John 4:7, 8.) "The Bible forbids physical or verbal spousal abuse. *It's in the Bible*, Colossians 3:19, NIV. 'Husbands, love your wives and do not be harsh with them.' "[9] The word *harsh* in the original Greek refers to being angry or bitter toward a partner; causing continued pain, intense hostility; and/or expressing hatred toward the other. Paul is clear that a spouse is not to be hostile or violent. Emotional, verbal, sexual, and/or physical abuse are not acceptable behavior for a Christian husband or wife. It is only acceptable to love your spouse.

In 1 Corinthians 13, Paul makes it clear that "love is patient, love is kind. It does not envy, it does not boast, it is not proud. It does not dishonor others, it is not self-seeking, it is not easily angered, it keeps no record of wrongs. Love does not delight in evil but rejoices with the truth. It always protects, always trusts, always hopes, always perseveres" (verses 4–7, NIV). Clearly, love's attributes do not remotely condone abuse.

A healthy relationship is one where both partners feel safe and protected, where anger is managed in a healthy way, and where serving one another is the norm. Often victims of abuse have feelings of guilt; as if they were responsible for provoking their abuser or perhaps were deserving of the abuse they received. Abusers can be controlling and skillful at making their victims feel responsible. The truth is that no one deserves to be abused by another, and abusers are responsible for their own choices and actions. The good news is that the Bible offers comfort—not guilt—for the victims of abuse. (Take the time to read and consider Psalm 91:1–16.)

Forgiveness and peace

"Forgiveness is basically a choice that we make to destroy that roadblock" to peace. In fact, "Jesus died to tear down the roadblocks caused by our sin," blockades we have built against Him, "and we are required to do the same for those who wrong us (Matthew 6:15)."[10] "Treat others as you want them to treat you. This is what the Law and the Prophets are all about" (Matthew 7:12, CEV).

Even if the relationship is not fully restored, it is important that we forgive. Sometimes we are told, "You need to forgive and forget," or "You need to forgive and seek reconciliation." These truisms may sound nice, but are they safe advice for the person who is being or who has been abused? Probably not. What matters most is the beauty of forgiveness and the freedom it brings to the person offering it, even when the relationship must end due to abuse or violence.

Jesus said, "I am giving you a new command. You must love each other, just as I have loved you" (John 13:34, CEV). This is not an option, a suggestion, or a consideration; it is His command to us. Though reconciliation may not be possible in every situation, forgiveness is always necessary.

For further consideration

1. Is it possible to have unity in the church while having negative feelings toward one another? What guidance does the Bible provide? See Romans 12:16; Philippians 1:27; 2:2; 1 Peter 3:8.

2. There is a proverb that says, "That which angers you controls you." How can you learn to control your anger before this happens?

3. While some conflict may go unresolved, we can still live in harmony with others. Our differences do not have to divide us. What can we do to ensure that, in spite of our differences, we remain united in the common cause of the gospel?

---

1. Ellen G. White, *Patriarchs and Prophets* (Mountain View, CA: Pacific Press®, 1958), 82.

2. Linda Ray, "How to Avoid Family Conflict," LiveStrong.com, July 10, 2015, https://www.livestrong.com/article/210548-how-to-avoid-family-conflict/.

3. Ray, "How to Avoid Family Conflict."

4. Ellen G. White, *The Acts of the Apostles* (Mountain View, CA: Pacific Press®, 1911), 305.

5. Mary J. Yerkes, "Destructive Conflict: Recognize It. Stop It," Focus on the Family, accessed August 21, 2018, https://www.focusonthefamily.com/lifechallenges/relationship-challenges/conflict-resolution/destructive-conflict-recognize-it-stop-it.

6. Yerkes, "Destructive Conflict."

7. Yerkes, "Destructive Conflict."

8. Kat White, "Receive Your Freedom From Anger," Işık Abla Ministries, accessed August 21, 2018, https://isikabla.com/receive-your-freedom-from-anger/.

9. "Abuse," Bibleinfo.com, accessed August 21, 2018, http://www.bibleinfo.com/en/topics/abuse; emphasis in the original.

10. "Forgiveness and Reconciliation," Great Bible Study.com, accessed August 21, 2018, http://www.greatbiblestudy.com/forgiveness.php.

CHAPTER 11

Seasons of Faith

Second Samuel records the tragic death of Absalom, King David's son, at the hand of Joab. In the chaotic aftermath, someone needed to give David the news that his son—and enemy—was now dead, making it safe for him to return to Jerusalem. When Joab commissioned an Ethiopian (a Cushite) to carry the sad news, there was another young man named Ahimaaz who, for some reason, wanted to be the one to tell the king. Joab had already dispatched the Cushite; but after much insistence on his part, Ahimaaz was also allowed to run to the king. Ahimaaz must have been an amazing athlete, for the Bible tells us that he caught up with the Ethiopian, passed him, and reached David first, far ahead of the Cushite.

When Ahimaaz reached the king, who was anxiously awaiting news about Absalom, he told the king that his enemies had been defeated. David pressed him for more information:

"Is my son Absalom all right?" David asked.
    Ahimaaz said, "When Joab sent your personal servant and me, I saw a noisy crowd. But I don't know what it was all about" (2 Samuel 18:29, CEV).

Family Seasons

The Cushite arrived just a few seconds later and, responding to the king's inquiry, said, "I wish that all Your Majesty's enemies and everyone who tries to harm you would end up like him!" (verse 32, CEV). David received the devastating news as any loving parent would. He "started trembling. Then he went up to the room above the city gate to cry. As he went, he kept saying, 'My son Absalom! My son, my son Absalom! I wish I could have died instead of you! Absalom, my son, my son!' " (verse 33, CEV).

We have always found this story fascinating. Why did Ahimaaz want to run to the king when he had no real news to share? It seems like sometimes we are so anxious to say or do something that we forget to have a goal or a message in mind. The author of the book of Hebrews uses a footrace to illustrate the life and ministry of Christ's followers. He says, "We must be determined to run the race that is ahead of us. We must keep our eyes on Jesus, who leads us and makes our faith complete" (Hebrews 12:1, 2, CEV). Our race is not physical; it is a faith-based race. It is a race alongside Jesus and toward His return.

In some ways, we marvel at Ahimaaz's passion for running and his desire to bear the good news of victory. Families of faith need both. Having a common message, a common goal, and a common ministry leads us to enjoy a strong faith.

In the years after World War II, when the children of returning soldiers grew into what is known as the baby boomer generation, churches began to look for ways to reach and retain the vast numbers of children and young people flocking to their congregations. Some churches decided to hire full-time, specialized pastors to organize children's programs and events. Seeing the success youth pastors were having, some churches moved to hire children's pastors. Little by little, the responsibility of discipling children was inadvertently taken from the parents and given to specialized ministries. We are not implying that having these ministries caused young people to stop attending church; rather, we see parents neglecting their God-given duties as the root cause. Too many parents rely on the church to raise and disciple their children, when the primary responsibility rests on their shoulders.

Ellen White wrote the following:

> After faithful labor, if you are satisfied that your children understand the meaning of conversion and baptism and are truly converted, let them be baptized. But, I repeat, first of all prepare yourselves to act as faithful shepherds in guiding their inexperienced feet in the narrow way of obedience. God must work in the parents that they may give to their children a right example in love, courtesy, and Christian humility, and in an entire giving up of self to Christ. If you consent to the baptism of your children and then leave them to do as they choose, feeling no special duty to keep their feet in the straight path, yourselves are responsible if they lose faith and courage and interest in the truth.[1]

Several things are clear from these words. First, it is the parents' responsibility to prepare their children for baptism, not the pastor's or the schoolteacher's. Second, the parents' work of disciple making continues after baptism. Third, disciple making is not simply teaching but leading by example "in love, courtesy, and Christian humility, and in an entire giving up of self to Christ." One of the best and most effective ways to transmit our faith to our children is through family ministry—parents and children participating together in acts of service.

Hold fast what is good—the ministry of the Word

The early Christian church recognized the apostles could not both preach the Word of God and help distribute food to those in need (Acts 6:1–6). In order to allow the apostles to devote themselves to "prayer and to the ministry of the word," the church selected and commissioned the first seven deacons (verse 4; see also verses 5, 6). "From the very earliest time in the church it was understood that the ministry of the Word required so much time and effort that those called to this ministry should be freed from other demands."[2] Paul taught Timothy that "the church should value the ministry of the Word so highly" that it should bear the responsibility of paying leaders who devote their lives to full-time ministry (1 Timothy 5:17, 18).

The ministry of the Word is not simply standing up to deliver a speech in church. The person who ministers the Word of God to others must first be a student of the Bible. God's hand was "upon Ezra, the Scripture says, because he 'had set his heart to *study the law of the Lord*, and to do it, and to teach his statutes and ordinances in Israel' (Ezra 7:9–10). And Paul tells Timothy to be zealous to present himself to God as a workman who does not need to be ashamed because he rightly handles the word of truth (2 Timothy 2:15)." "The ministry of the Word is [also] a ministry of prayer." (See Proverbs 2:3–5.)[3]

Families and church families have their differences because their backgrounds and life experiences vary. In the modern global community, we even come from different cultures. Paul and his colleagues in ministry also experienced some of these differences as they traveled on their missionary journeys. Knowing the divisions that would challenge the church, Paul wrote to encourage the believers in Rome: "Be sincere in your love for others. Hate everything that is evil and hold tight to everything that is good" (Romans 12:9, CEV).

For Paul and today's parents, it is important that children in the faith hold on to all that is good. Paul also wrote to the struggling believers in Corinth: "My friends, I want you to remember the message that I preached and that you believed and trusted. You will be saved by this message, if you hold firmly to it. But if you don't, your faith was all for nothing" (1 Corinthians 15:1, 2, CEV). And he admonished the Thessalonians, "Prove all things; hold fast that which is good" (1 Thessalonians 5:21, ASV). Four times we read in the book of Hebrews to "hold fast our confidence and our boasting in our hope" (Hebrews 3:6, ESV), "hold fast our confession" (Hebrews 4:14, ESV), "hold fast to the hope set before us" (Hebrews 6:18, ESV), and "hold fast the confession of our hope without wavering, for he who promised is faithful" (Hebrews 10:23, ESV).

The power of culture in our family

Everyone is affected by their culture, even those who lived in Abraham's time. After the destruction of Sodom and Gomorrah, Lot fled to Zoar. But realizing that the evils he had witnessed in his old home were present even there, "Lot made his way to the mountains, and abode in a cave, stripped of all for which he had dared to subject his family to the influences of a wicked city. But the curse of Sodom followed him even here. The sinful conduct of his daughters was the result of the evil associations of that vile place. Its moral corruption had become so interwoven with their character that they could not distinguish between good and evil."[4]

Centuries later, culture continued to have an adverse influence on the church. "In 313 CE, Constantine the Great . . . ended the sporadic-yet-terrifying Christian persecutions under the Roman Empire with his 'Edict of Milan,' and brought the Christian church under imperial protection. Not surprisingly, public social activities and normative culture changed . . . for the early Christians." Unfortunately, "a new cultural permissiveness and secularism arose with the faith; and pious believers began to worry more about church immorality, abuse, and vice."[5] These concerns led to the beginning of the monastic lifestyle.

"This Christian monastic movement was simple at first, but, as is common to all societies, its routine became more and more convoluted" and fanatical. As a result, "one could find monks and nuns in caves, in the swamp, in a cemetery, and even 12 metres (40 feet) up on stylite [a pillar]," to show their rejection of the world and its practices.[6]

Should we follow suit and move our families to deserts or isolated mountains, maintaining little or no contact with the outside world? Would such a move keep our children pure and undefiled from the world's influences? This quest for holiness is one that some have embraced on the strength of Jesus' own words: "If you belonged to the world, its people would love you. But you don't belong to the world. I have chosen you to leave the world behind, and that is why its people hate you" (John 15:19, CEV). Yet Jesus understood that one can be *in* the world without participating in what the world does: "I have told them [the disciples] your [God's] message. But the people of this world hate them, because they don't belong to this world, just as I don't" (John 17:14, CEV).

Understanding this tension, Paul wrote to the church in Rome: "Dear friends, God is good. So I beg you to offer your bodies to him as a living sacrifice, pure and pleasing. That's the most sensible way to serve God. Don't be like the people of this world, but let God change the way you think. Then you will know how to do everything that is good and pleasing to him" (Romans 12:1, 2, CEV).

Toward a first-generation faith

It has been said that God does not have grandchildren. This means that while we should transmit our faith to our children, God accepts every person individually as His son or daughter. We do not receive adoption into the family through someone else. Each believer is a first-generation Christian. We cannot simply be acculturated into the faith, living it because that is the way we were raised, because it is comfortable, or because it is all we know. Being cultural Christians is not enough to sustain us, much less transmit our faith to the next generation.

> How long does it take to lose a culture, from a Christian perspective?
> Actually, it takes only one generation.
> . . . Adolf Hitler understood this when he said, "He alone, who owns the youth, gains the future!" [Adolf Hitler, quoted in Office of United States Chief of Counsel for

Prosecution of Axis Criminality, *Nazi Conspiracy and Aggression*, vol. 1 (Washington, DC: United States Government Printing Office, 1946), 320].

Over and over again in Scripture, God instructs His people to make sure they train up the next generation.[7]

On one such occasion, before God led the children of Israel through the Jordan River to the Promised Land, He told Joshua to take twelve stones from the middle of the dried-up riverbed and build a memorial on the other side of the Jordan. Why was God so intent on having the monument built?[8] Joshua explained the significance to the people, "Years from now your children will ask you why these rocks are here. Tell them, 'The Lord our God dried up the Jordan River so we could walk across. He did the same thing here for us that he did for our people at the Red Sea, because he wants everyone on earth to know how powerful he is. And he wants us to worship only him' " (Joshua 4:21–24, CEV).

The stones were there to teach future generations about the true God. Parents would reference them as they passed along a knowledge of God to their children. Such powerful reminders should have been enough, but one of the saddest passages in the Scriptures tells us, "After a while the people of Joshua's generation died, and the next generation did not know the Lord or any of the things he had done for Israel. The Lord had brought their ancestors out of Egypt, and they had worshiped him. But now the Israelites stopped worshiping the Lord and worshiped the idols of Baal and Astarte, as well as the idols of other gods from nearby nations" (Judges 2:10, 11, CEV). "It took only one generation to lose the spiritual legacy that should have been passed on."[9]

How could this happen? Perhaps the parents in that generation forgot the words of Moses: "Listen, Israel! The Lord our God is the only true God! So love the Lord your God with all your heart, soul, and strength. Memorize his laws and tell them to your children over and over again. Talk about them all the time, whether you're at home or walking along the road or going to bed at night, or getting up in the morning. Write down copies and tie them to your wrists and foreheads to help you obey them. Write these laws on the door frames of your homes and on your town gates" (Deuteronomy 6:4–9, CEV).

It seems the parents of Joshua's day failed to teach their children about God, and in just one generation, the nation became wayward! It is grace that ultimately saves anyone, but God has bequeathed to parents the responsibility of teaching their children about the gift of salvation—both its conditions and its rewards.[10]

What a privilege to help successive generations become first-generation children of God and disciples of Jesus. God wants our children to do better than Ahimaaz, running without any real news, much less good news. Instead, He wants them to be runners with purpose and a message, making disciples of all nations and teaching them about the wonders of an eternal relationship with Jesus Christ.

For further consideration

1. If ministry is not limited to full-time pastors, teachers, evangelists, and missionaries, what role does the average church member play in the church's mission?

2. What spiritual "stones of remembrance" does your family share? How can these memories strengthen the faith of your children?

---

1. Ellen G. White, *Child Guidance* (Washington, DC: Review and Herald®, 1954), 500.

2. John Piper, "The Ministry of the Word: Ordination of Steve Roy," Desiring God, accessed August 21, 2018, https://www.desiringgod.org/messages/the-ministry-of-the-word.

3. Piper, "The Ministry of the Word"; emphasis in the original.

4. Ellen G. White, *Patriarchs and Prophets* (Mountain View, CA: Pacific Press®, 1958), 167, 168.

5. John S. Knox, "The Monastic Movement: Origins & Purposes," Ancient History Encyclopedia, August 23, 2016, https://www.ancient.eu/article/930/the-monastic-movement-origins--purposes/.

6. Knox, "The Monastic Movement."

7. Ken Ham, "Gone in Only One Generation: Battle for Kids' Minds," Answers in Genesis, January 1, 2013, https://answersingenesis.org/culture/gone-in-only-one-generation/#fn_1.
8. Ham, "Gone in Only One Generation."
9. Ham, "Gone in Only One Generation."
10. Ham, "Gone in Only One Generation."

CHAPTER 12

Seasons of Witnessing

At Jesus' ascension, He gave His disciples what we now call the gospel commission: "Go to the people of all nations and make them my disciples. Baptize them in the name of the Father, the Son, and the Holy Spirit, and teach them to do everything I have told you. I will be with you always, even until the end of the world" (Matthew 28:19, 20, CEV). This statement demonstrates that baptism, disciple making, witnessing, and evangelism are closely linked concepts. They form the fundamentals of Christianity and represent distinct experiences in the Christian's life.

Without getting too technical, we will simply say that *disciple making* is teaching others, through word and example, how to be followers of Jesus (Matthew 11:28-30); *witnessing* is telling others what God has done for us (Mark 5:19); and *evangelism* is telling others the good news of God's salvation (Matthew 24:14). The lines of distinction are often blurred, so we will not labor over the differences. What is important to understand is that all people are called to share the good news of what God has done for them and how He can do the same for those who wish to become His children and disciples. The gospel commission, given to those gathered at His ascension, is also our commission and our homes are the first mission fields.

Family Seasons

What have they seen in your house?

Ellen White expressed the witnessing lifestyle best when she wrote the following:

> Our work for Christ is to begin with the family in the home. . . . There is no missionary field more important than this. By precept and example parents are to teach their children to labor for the unconverted. The children should be so educated that they will sympathize with the aged and afflicted and will seek to alleviate the sufferings of the poor and distressed. They should be taught to be diligent in missionary work; and from their earliest years self-denial and sacrifice for the good of others and the advancement of Christ's cause should be inculcated, that they may be laborers together with God.
>
> But if they ever learn to do genuine missionary work for others, they must first learn to labor for those at home, who have a natural right to their offices of love.[1]

A careful study of the words above reveals specific ideas on witnessing and disciple making in the home:

1. *By precept and example*: Children need to be taught about respect, boundaries, responsibility, civility, and sympathy. But it is even more important that these values are demonstrated in the parents' lives, not just taught through their words.
2. *Diligence, self-denial, and sacrifice*: We teach our children about giving through such songs as "A Boat Goes Sailing." We do so because we believe it is important that they learn about the opportunities to reach people for Jesus in faraway places. Helping them to understand the blessings of service to others is crucial for their spiritual health. Though young, they can learn the benefits and joys of doing without for the good of others.

3. *Working for those at home*: The primary sphere of influence is the home where the children live. To reinforce this idea, Ellen White notes that if children "ever learn to do genuine missionary work for others, they must first learn to labor for those at home, who have a natural right to their offices of love."[2]

Everyone in the family needs to appreciate that the home is the most important mission field in the world. At the same time, they must also learn that it is not the only mission field. Ellen White states, "The mission of the home extends beyond its own members. The Christian home is to be an object lesson, illustrating the excellence of the true principles of life. Such an illustration will be a power for good in the world. . . . As the youth go out from such a home, the lessons they have learned are imparted. Nobler principles of life are introduced into other households, and an uplifting influence works in the community."[3] Having learned and practiced mission and service at home, family members can then witness to others outside the home. People do not need to see a perfect family; they are most impressed by an authentic one where love, kindness, and commitment fragrance the entire family unit.

Family first

In retelling Israel's experience of leaving Egypt, Moses provides one of the earliest parenting messages found in Scripture. His words were not directed to the Levites or the leaders of the tribes, or even to the entire group of former slaves. His words were given directly to parents: "Listen, Israel! The LORD our God is the only true God! So love the LORD your God with all your heart, soul, and strength. Memorize his laws and tell them to your children over and over again. Talk about them all the time, whether you're at home or walking along the road or going to bed at night, or getting up in the morning. Write down copies and tie them to your wrists and foreheads to help you obey them. Write these laws on the door frames of your homes and on your town gates" (Deuteronomy 6:4–9, CEV). It is imperative that parents follow these steps as they transmit their faith to their children:

1. *First of all, love the Lord.* Note that parents must first love the Lord themselves. God asks for their entire commitment to Him—heart, soul, and strength. The love of Jesus must be in parents before it can be transmitted to their children.
2. *Study His Word and commit it to memory.* Before parents can communicate God's truth to their children, they must study His Word and spend time with Him daily. Jesus must be their personal Savior before He can be introduced to their children.
3. *Then begin to teach the Word to your children.* The teaching Moses has in mind is not an occasional reading of selected passages from the Bible, Sabbath School lesson, or a children's study guide. It is through family interactions in daily life and practicing biblical principles in the home that children come to know and love Jesus as their God.

Peace that wins—the mission of marriage

For many around the world, marriage is simply a social arrangement. In other areas, people marry because they are in love, are lonely, or have financial needs. Still others marry to secure better health and a longer life. In the Bible, however, marriage is a symbol of the relationship that exists between Jesus, the Groom, and the church, His bride (Ephesians 5:25–32; Revelation 22:17).

In Ephesians, Paul presents a beautiful image of marriage. He explains that Jesus loved His bride, the church, so much that He gave Himself completely for her, dying on the cross to present her to Himself pure, without spot or wrinkle (see Ephesians 5:26, 27). Using this image of the loving relationship between Jesus and His bride, Paul goes on to admonish husbands to view their wives in the same way. In other words, Paul is telling husbands that their mission on earth is to help their wives in the process of sanctification—their preparation for Jesus' return.

Paul's message is important because marriage is about far more than procreation or fleeting happiness; it constitutes God's gift to make us holy. When Christian husbands and wives submit to the Lord and to each other, they become instruments of the Holy Spirit in the process of sanctification (Ephesians 5:21). "Marriage is a refining process that God will use to have us become the man or woman He wants us to become. Think about it. God will use your marriage for His purpose. He will mold and refine you for your own benefit and for His glory."[4] What a solemn responsibility rests on Christian husbands and wives—to help their spouses be ready for the return of Jesus. This mission and ministry explain Malachi's words: " 'For I hate divorce!' says the LORD, the God of Israel. 'To divorce your wife is to overwhelm her with cruelty,' says the LORD of Heaven's Armies" (Malachi 2:16, NLT). Divorce is a rejection of God's call to participate in the mission of a spouse's sanctification. It tragically harms people and pains God's heart.

Family life is for sharing

Strong marriages build strong families. These strong families understand the seasons of sharing joy because they live them regularly. A young woman anticipates the day she will become a bride, and when the day arrives, she shines with joy. When she holds her baby for the first time, nothing can contain her overflowing love. Jesus described the experience well when He told His disciples, "When a woman is about to give birth, she is in great pain. But after it is all over, she forgets the pain and is happy, because she has brought a child into the world" (John 16:21, CEV). As her son learns to walk and talk, he spontaneously shares his hugs, endearing him to the heart of his mother. As a father plays with his little girl, reads to her, and eventually attends her graduation, he is filled with pride at the beautiful and intelligent young woman she has become. All too soon, the cycle of life is complete, and the seasons of joy begin again.

Each year we rejoice during these special times. Birthdays celebrate creation, birth, and gratitude for one more year of life. Wedding anniversaries are reminders of life's journey—where we have been and how far God has brought us. These marvelous seasons of happiness are not limited to big events. Holidays bring us together to relax, reminisce, and laugh. Vacations offer rest, renewed energy, and new memories.

These events deepen friendships and create new joys. Paul also enjoyed good times with people and referenced it in his letter to Philemon. "My friend, your love has made me happy and has greatly encouraged me. It has also cheered the hearts of God's people" (Philemon 7, CEV). To his friends in Philippi, he penned these words: "Every time I think of you, I thank my God. And whenever I mention you in my prayers, it makes me happy" (Philippians 1:3, 4, CEV). It was true then and it is true today: family and friends bring immense joy and meaning to our lives and share moments that are memorable and sweet.

Centers of contagious friendliness

In a cold and lonely world, a loving touch, an open heart, or a welcoming home can be an oasis of heavenly bliss. *Hospitality* usually refers to opening one's home and sharing its comforts with others. The Bible says this godly characteristic is the mark of mature leadership (1 Timothy 3:2). Yet we often hold tightly to our possessions, even as God asks us to do otherwise. After all, everything we own comes from God (James 1:17; 1 Corinthians 4:7). He asks us to be generous with what we have received and to be hospitable (Matthew 10:8; Romans 12:5–8; Isaiah 58:6–11). He knows our tendencies to keep our possessions and hoard His blessings. Still, in His grace, He helps us to relax our grip on self-centeredness and share our lives and blessings with others.

> Even among those who profess to be Christians, true hospitality is little exercised. Among our own people the

opportunity of showing hospitality is not regarded as it should be, as a privilege and blessing. There is altogether too little sociability, too little of a disposition to make room for two or three more at the family board, without embarrassment or parade. Some plead that "it is too much trouble." It would not be if you would say, "We have made no special preparation, but you are welcome to what we have." By the unexpected guest a welcome is appreciated far more than is the most elaborate preparation.[5]

By all accounts, Ellen White's personality seems to have been warm, caring, and friendly. Given her responsibilities, along with travel and speaking appointments, she must have been a fairly outgoing person and comfortable around people. But she never set herself up as the norm for others' behavior.

Social scientists speak of two personality types: extroverts and introverts. "An extrovert is someone who recharges" his or her "energy from being around people. . . . [He or she] doesn't mind being alone, but prefers the company of others as it makes" the person happy and excited. It "doesn't mean that . . . [he or she is] good with people or happy all the time, but that other people's company is important" and energizes him or her. "An introvert is a person who is energized by spending time alone." They prefer "homes, libraries, quiet parks," and other secluded places with few people. "Contrary to popular belief, not all introverts are shy. Some may have great social lives and love talking to their friends but just need some time to be alone to 'recharge' afterwards."[6]

Naturally, socializing and hospitality are much easier for extroverts than they are for introverts. Nevertheless, introverts can be excellent listeners, and one on one, they can be a blessing to someone who needs a listening ear.

God created each of us with unique temperaments and personalities, capable of touching other lives in positive ways. Understanding these preferences and differences can strengthen our witness for God. While some are more sociable and enjoy entertaining strangers, others are better suited to quietly listen. Each person is uniquely gifted to help others and fulfill the gospel commission.

For further consideration

1. Consider your home and family life, then answer the following question: What have others seen in my home? What would your neighbors say about you?

2. Have you witnessed God's power? Do you tell others about His involvement in your life? Can you begin right now with the person or people closest to you?

3. Consider your personality type—extrovert or introvert. How can you practice hospitality in a way that brings you energy?

---

1. Ellen G. White, *Testimonies for the Church*, (Mountain View, CA: Pacific Press®, 1948), 6:429.

2. White, *Testimonies for the Church*, 6:429.

3. Ellen G. White, *The Adventist Home* (Washington, DC: Review and Herald®, 1952), 31.

4. H. Norman Wright and Wes Roberts, *Before You Say "I Do,"* rev. and expanded ed. (Eugene, OR: Harvest House, 1997), 8.

5. White, *Testimonies for the Church*, 6:343.

6. Magdalena, "Are You an Introvert?" *Small Town Blogger* (blog), February 17, 2015, https://smalltownfashionblogger.wordpress.com/2015/02/17/are-you-an-introvert/.

CHAPTER 13

The Final Season

Elijah, a prominent Old Testament prophet, is best known as a man of prayer. James, the author of the New Testament book that bears his name, was also a man of prayer and noted its power: "The earnest prayer of a righteous person has great power and produces wonderful results" (James 5:16, NLT). As proof of that declaration, James cites Elijah's powerful petition: "Elijah was as human as we are, and yet when he prayed earnestly that no rain would fall, none fell for three and a half years!" (verse 17, NLT).

"Elijah lived in a time when the foundations [of religion and society] were being destroyed. It was a time of spiritual apostasy and moral decay. The nation [of Israel] had abandoned God's law and turned to the worship of Baal." Elijah, James observes, "was as human as we are." He had the same passions, the same temptations, and the same struggles we have today. But "he was also a man of uncommon courage—a man willing to risk his life for the glory and cause of God."

"What gave Elijah this uncommon courage? Did the Lord appear to him in a dream, or speak to him from a bush as with Moses?" No, what we are told is that God revealed Himself to Elijah in "a less sensational but even more miraculous way"—the same way He wants to reveal Himself today. Just as He communed with Daniel during his daily prayers, God revealed Himself to Elijah as he spent time with Him. "His courage was the product of intimately knowing God and living in close fellowship with the Lord through the Word and prayer. In the process, God's purposes, burdens, values, and desires became engraved on his heart." "Convinced of God's answer" to his prayer, he could not help but boldly declare his message to King Ahab.[1]

Today, the Elijah message is more important than ever. Seventh-day Adventists need God's sanctified boldness and courage to stand up and speak against the forces threatening to destroy our children and us. Ellen White eloquently writes, "The greatest want of the world is the want of men—men who will not be bought or sold, men who in their inmost souls are true and honest, men who do not fear to call sin by its right name, men whose conscience is as true to duty as the needle to the pole, men who will stand for the right though the heavens fall."[2]

Turning hearts at the end

As the conquest of the Promised Land reached its conclusion, Joshua, also at the end of his life and career, challenged the people: "But if you don't want to worship the LORD, then choose right now! Will you worship the same idols your ancestors did? Or since you're living on land that once belonged to the Amorites, maybe you'll worship their gods. I won't. My family and I are going to worship and obey the LORD!" (Joshua 24:15, CEV). His message, like Elijah's, was a message of hearth and home—a challenge to leave the ordinary and turn toward God. His call to the Israelites, God's chosen people, was to become spiritual Israel.

We hear the same call today; it is a call to worship God and join spiritual Israel with all our hearts. Here are some ideas on how modern families can act on Joshua's call and enjoy fellowship in God's spiritual family:

1. A spiritual family worships together. A spiritual family chooses to attend church and be engaged with fellow believers. They must also make daily worship a part of their lives.

2. A spiritual family honors God's Word and applies it in their home. A spiritual family recognizes that God's Word "is a lamp that gives light wherever . . . [they] walk" (Psalm 119:105, CEV). Parents should heed Moses' instruction regarding God's commandments: "Recite them to your children and talk about them when you are at home and when you are away, when you lie down and when you rise" (Deuteronomy 6:7, NRSV).

3. Spiritual families make prayer a daily part of their home lives. Many people are familiar with the slogan, "The family that prays together, stays together." How true! It is difficult to find a family that has prayed together on a daily basis that breaks down and falls apart. If you want your family to stay together, then pray together. Some have observed that a prayerless family is a powerless family.[3]

In Colossians 1:9–14, the apostle Paul outlines how to pray for those we love. You can easily use these seven requests as you seek God on behalf of your loved ones.

1. Pray that they will know God's will (verse 9).
2. Pray that they will walk in a way that is worthy (verse 10).
3. Pray that their lives will be fruitful (verse 10).
4. Pray that they will hunger to know God (verse 10).
5. Pray that they will be strong and mighty (verse 11).
6. Pray that they will be patient, persistent, and joyous (verse 11).
7. Pray that they will express thanks each day for the three greatest gifts in life (verses 12–14). And what are the three greatest gifts? The forgiveness of sin, the deliverance from sin, and entrance to the kingdom of God.

Like Joshua's call to ancient Israel, the Elijah message is more than a call to repentance and preparation for the second coming of Jesus. It is also a call for families to return to God and worship Him alone.

Family Seasons

The drama of the ages will soon close, and Ellen White offers a grand description of the family reunion that will take place: "The living righteous are changed 'in a moment, in the twinkling of an eye.' At the voice of God they were glorified; now they are made immortal and with the risen saints are caught up to meet their Lord in the air. Angels 'gather together His elect from the four winds, from one end of heaven to the other.' Little children are borne by holy angels to their mothers' arms. Friends long separated by death are united, nevermore to part, and with songs of gladness ascend together to the City of God."[4] This moment will undoubtedly be the greatest family reunion the world has ever seen. What are we waiting for?

Renewal at the family altar

Now back to the message to Ahab in 1 Kings 17:1. This verse contains three declarations that shed light on Elijah's faith and courage and the spiritual condition of his heart. Certainly, he was full of God's love and "if we want to understand this man and learn from his example, we need to examine these powerful, revealing words."[5] These words are worth noting because Jesus reminds us, "Out of the abundance of the heart the mouth speaks" (Matthew 12:34, NRSV).

1. "As the LORD, the God of Israel lives" (1 Kings 17:1, NASB). Elijah was convinced that God was a real person, not a fictional character like Santa Claus or a man-made idol "of gold and silver and bronze and stone and wood, which cannot see or hear or walk" (Revelation 9:20, ESV). Elijah shared Job's confidence, who in the midst of his losses boldly proclaimed, "I know that my Redeemer lives, and at the last he will stand upon the earth" (Job 19:25, ESV).

2. "Before whom I stand" (1 Kings 17:1, NASB). Elijah recognized God's person and His presence. God is not "watching us from a distance," as Bette Midler sings.[6] He is near us, next to us, especially when we walk through the furnace of trials (see Daniel 3). We may not always hear Him, but it is not because He is not there. As British writer C. S. Lewis writes, "God whispers to us in our pleasures, speaks in our conscience, but shouts in our pain."[7] Elijah, Daniel, Shadrach, Meshach, Abed-Nego, Paul, and countless other champions of faith lived heroically in the face of persecution. They knew God personally and felt His presence in their lives.

3. *"Surely there shall be neither dew nor rain these years, except by my word" (1 Kings 17:1, NASB).* Elijah "was confident in God's promises." Keep in mind that "the prophets of Baal claimed Baal-Melqart was the god of thunder, rain, and good crops. Elijah's declaration in 1 Kings 17:1 strongly challenged the reality of their god and their faith. It showed Baal was false and impotent." On the other hand, Elijah's words "showed truth and salvation could only be found in the prophets of Yahweh."[8] Elijah reminds us that simply talking about God and His power is not enough; we need to live accordingly. The New Testament reiterates this: "You know these things, and God will bless you, if you do them" (John 13:17, CEV). "The people who are really blessed are the ones who hear and obey God's message!" (Luke 11:28, CEV).

The declarations that God lives, that He is present, and that His promises are trustworthy sum up our beliefs. They must be transmitted to our children from their earliest days, ensuring that the next generation makes them their own. That is why today's family worship time is as important as the altar in Elijah's day. Worship, study, and prayer—in the morning and the evening—provide safe bookends for the daily lives of every family. To be distracted and neglect these precious minutes together increases the risk of worshiping false idols instead of devoting ourselves to the one and only true God.

Trust God with your family

Sometimes bleak circumstances make it difficult to trust God with the future. To allay our fears, the Old Testament includes the story of Elijah's encounter with the widow of Zarephath. There are at least three lessons to be learned from this story.

Family Seasons

1. The biblical record states that this widow was specially selected by God: "The LORD told Elijah, 'Go to the town of Zarephath in Sidon and live there. I've told a widow in that town to give you food' " (1 Kings 17:8, 9, CEV). Jesus made it clear that "there were many widows in Israel, but Elijah was sent only to a widow in the town of Zarephath near the city of Sidon" (Luke 4:25, 26, CEV).

Take a moment and read the account in 1 Kings 17:8–16. No one can argue that God's choice of this widow was unfair—she was at the end of her rope and He was coming to her rescue. Even so, it is interesting that His deliverance of this widow involved acts of service on her part. She was not simply selected to be saved from the famine; she was chosen to serve God's greater purpose for Elijah and Israel. She could hardly understand the implications of trusting God at the worst moment of her life, but she was first and foremost a woman of faith. Acting on this faith, she courageously made the little cake for Elijah first, providing for the needs of the prophet. Only then did she experience the multiplication of the meal and oil.

2. God communicates with us but not always with words. The story says that God commanded this widow to give Elijah some food, but we are not told when, where, or how He did it. Somehow God must have worked on her heart and mind, impressing her to go out and gather sticks for the last meal with her son. Maybe you, too, have had the experience of being "moved" to do something you did not think much about or did not completely understand at the time, later realizing it was God moving in your life. An impression to go someplace, do something, or act in a certain way suddenly becomes significant when you learn that you unknowingly impacted someone's life. It is exhilarating to think that the Holy Spirit is leading us to do God's will; He knows best where He needs to take us.

3. This story teaches that the widow of Zarephath was a willing instrument of God. Here is a woman selected to sustain the prophet, not from a position of abundance but one of poverty.

The Final Season

When God called Moses, he responded with four excuses for his noncompliance. When God came to Isaiah, he said, "I am too sinful." When God approached Jeremiah, he demurred, "I am too young." When God summoned Amos, he balked, "I do not have the qualifications." Not to mention Jonah and his ill-fated flight from God's will. But this poor widow, who had nothing but a bit of flour and oil, a few sticks, and one son, willingly obeyed God's invitation to participate in the prophet's mission.

An important footnote for today's families is this: God intervenes in the most unexpected ways. Elijah could not hide anywhere in Israel because the king was hunting him; he needed to flee to another country. Queen Jezebel was from Sidon, and if anyone found out Elijah was there, he would be captured. But of all people, God prepared a widow living just on the border to care for the prophet. We would not have come up with that plan, but God found a widow whose very insignificance and poverty actually led to the safety of the prophet.

Sometimes God waits until we are at our limit, our breaking point, before unexpectedly and miraculously stepping in on our behalf. How sweet it is to rest in His providence, knowing He has servants everywhere. He understands each difficulty we face and is working to accomplish His will in our lives. The seasons vary, but His love does not.

For further consideration

1. If you are a parent, in what ways can you make your devotional times more meaningful for your children? Is the worship age appropriate?

2. Think of a time in your life when God intervened and worked in an amazing way. This experience is part of your testimony. Have you ever shared it with anyone? Ask God to lead you to someone who needs to hear your story.

---

1. J. Hampton Keathley III, "3. The Message of Elijah (1 King 17:1)," Bible.org, June 4, 2004, https://bible.org/seriespage/message-elijah-1-kings-171.

Family Seasons

2. Ellen G. White, *Education* (Mountain View, CA: Pacific Press®, 1903), 57.

3. Adapted from Claudio Consuegra and Pamela Consuegra, "Building a Healthy Home," in *Discipleship and Service: Reaching Families for Jesus*, ed. Willie Oliver and Elaine Oliver (Silver Spring, MD: General Conference of Seventh-day Adventists, 2017), 47, http://bit.ly/FM2018PlanbookENG.

4. Ellen G. White, *Child Guidance* (Washington, DC: Review and Herald®, 1954), 566.

5. Keathley, "The Message of Elijah."

6. Julie Gold, "From a Distance," (New York: BMI, 1985), http://www.songfacts.com/detail.php?lyrics=4273.

7. C. S. Lewis, *The Problem of Pain*, rev. ed. (New York: HarperOne, 2015), 91.

8. Keathley, "The Message of Elijah."

EPILOGUE

Eternity With Jesus

For everything there is a season, and a time for every matter under heaven:

> a time to be born, and a time to die;
> a time to plant, and a time to pluck up what is planted;
> a time to kill, and a time to heal;
> a time to break down, and a time to build up;
> a time to weep, and a time to laugh;
> a time to mourn, and a time to dance;
> a time to cast away stones, and a time to gather stones together;
> a time to embrace, and a time to refrain from embracing;
> a time to seek, and a time to lose;
> a time to keep, and a time to cast away;
> a time to tear, and a time to sew;
> a time to keep silence, and a time to speak;
> a time to love, and a time to hate;
> a time for war, and a time for peace (Ecclesiastes 3:1–8, ESV).

When God re-creates the earth, the "seasons" will change.

Family Seasons

There will no longer be a time for war, death, hatred, and weeping. There will only be time for laughter, peace, worship, and life eternal. The existence of the redeemed will never again be marred by sin and the tragic consequences of hatred, death, and sorrow.

> The LORD has taken away the judgments against you;
>   he has cleared away your enemies.
> The King of Israel, the LORD, is in your midst;
>   you shall never again fear evil (Zephaniah 3:15, ESV).

In this everlasting season of peace,

> Surely goodness and mercy shall follow me
> All the days of my life;
> And I will dwell in the house of the LORD
> Forever (Psalm 23:6).

There will be work, most pleasant and fruitful: "They shall build houses and inhabit them; they shall plant vineyards and eat their fruit" (Isaiah 65:21). Children will not have to visit zoos:

> "The wolf also shall dwell with the lamb,
> The leopard shall lie down with the young goat,
> The calf and the young lion and the fatling together;
> And a little child shall lead them" (Isaiah 11:6).

At long last, the season of spending eternity with Jesus will finally come to every family.